HERITAGE
Crochet
In A New Light

Enriching Your Designs with Heirloom Lace Techniques

Rita de Maintenon

Schiffer Publishing Ltd

4880 Lower Valley Road • Atglen, PA 19310

Other Schiffer Books on Related Subjects:

From Thread and Wire: 60 Jewelry Projects Using Knitting and Crocheting, Helga Becker, photos by Helga and Richard Becker, ISBN 978-0-7643-4976-8

Artistry in Fiber, Vol. 2: Sculpture, Anne Lee, E. Ashley Rooney, foreword by Lois Russell, introduction by Adrienne Sloane, ISBN 978-0-7643-5342-0

Patchwork Knitting: 18 Projects to Knit and Crochet, Johanna Schwarz, ISBN 978-0-7643-4092-5

Copyright © 2017 by Rita de Maintenon

Library of Congress Control Number: 2017939840

Cover design by Danielle Farmer
Type set in Adobe Jenson Pro/Times New Roman

ISBN: 978-0-7643-5347-5
Printed in China

Published by Schiffer Publishing, Ltd.
4880 Lower Valley Road
Atglen, PA 19310
Phone: (610) 593-1777; Fax: (610) 593-2002
E-mail: Info@schifferbooks.com
Web: www.schifferbooks.com

For our complete selection of fine books on this and related subjects, please visit our website at www.schifferbooks.com. You may also write for a free catalog.

Schiffer Publishing's titles are available at special discounts for bulk purchases for sales promotions or premiums. Special editions, including personalized covers, corporate imprints, and excerpts, can be created in large quantities for special needs. For more information, contact the publisher.

We are always looking for people to write books on new and related subjects. If you have an idea for a book, please contact us at proposals@schifferbooks.com.

This book is dedicated to all crocheters who want to venture beyond the basics and design their own lace creations. It aims to inspire intermediate and advanced fiber artists to preserve the past in contemporary designs.

"Gold leaf was hammered out and cut into threads to work into the blue, purple and crimson linens…in skilled designs."
—Exodus 39:3

CONTENTS

ACKNOWLEDGMENTS

With thanks to Steward Stokes for the use of his photographs, Susan Taylor for her help in editing this book, and David Debs for technical and moral support.

PREFACE

Welcome to *Heritage Crochet in a New Light*! Thank you for your willingness to join me in the adventure of exploring many of our heritage techniques in a more updated, contemporary application.

Many good books have been written on the subject of individual lace techniques and there are lots of vintage and new patterns available. This book offers a personal journey into folklore, research, and my stubborn persistence to be pattern independent. Mostly I would like to encourage you, the reader, to experiment with combining several techniques in one particular designer piece. When I show you how to easily flow from one technique to another, you will see that they beg to be worked together.

Often when I demonstrate these techniques someone comes up to me and shares that their grandmother or some long-lost relative used to crochet and that some even used the tools laid out on my table. When they take a closer look as well as time for conversation, they realize that my work is different due to unusual use and combinations of our basic techniques. Although my grandmother taught me, this is not Grandma's crochet anymore! My personal mission is to preserve the past and to carry it forward in more contemporary and creative ways.

In this book I will give you some historical background about each technique, often handed down through generations—and folklore—here in the USA and in Europe. I have done in-depth research on the origins of each technique, and encourage you to explore further. Confirming these origins, using many generations of often incompletely-documented information, is not an exact science.

Each chapter is dedicated to a particular skill, with the emphasis on the basic rules required to master it. None of the techniques presented here are very difficult once you are comfortable with basic crochet skills and observe the golden rules of left hand tension (see below) and watch the numbers, which means counting stitches when needed. I still count after decades of playing with loops and stitches, and you will eventually become very comfortable with precise work. This will enable you to practice pattern independency when creating your own designs.

To keep your practice work interesting and offer encouragement to become your own designer, I will include suggestions on how to combine different techniques and which ones work well together so you can freely move from one technique to another once you master the basic concepts. In the last chapter I will give you the design secrets that allow you to create your own heirloom treasures.

A word about commercial patterns: They can be a great guide for beginners to get their feet wet, if they are written clearly and accurately. Most requests for help—from beginners and experienced crocheters alike—are about patterns. I have seldom been comfortable limiting myself to working from a pattern and, just as with using a recipe from a cookbook, I might look at it and then create a dish based on the suggestion, not the rules. You can do the same when crocheting, and practice pattern independency.

Be sure to keep a notepad and calculator handy as you work along with me. Other tools needed are sharp scissors, a measuring tape, and a metal darning needle. I also use a bright overhead light; it really saves my eyes as I work and keeps me from squinting.

So by now you know that this is not a book of patterns. There are directions on how to master the techniques, and suggestions on how you might use them in a way that will personally appeal to you. Here and there, I share a pattern to help you on your road to creativity.

Are you ready for a creative journey into the world of heritage crochet? Then let's bring out your inner fiber artist together.

"I do what I love and I love what I do."

To help and inspire you as you use this book, there are how-to videos on my website. Visit:

www.heirloomtreasuresfiberarts.com

INTRODUCTION

Before we venture into the heritage techniques I would like to emphasize a few important basics.

My instructions are written for right-handed crocheters; if you are left-handed, please use the mirror system and reverse the instructions.

The proper left hand tension and mastering of the very basics are essential to success in our journey through this book. I will use clear language and few abbreviations and will trust that you are comfortable with your slip knot, foundation chain, single crochet, half double crochet, and double crochet. If you are a bit rusty, I recommend that you do a swatch of these basics to refresh and prepare your mind for the fun to come.

So let's begin:

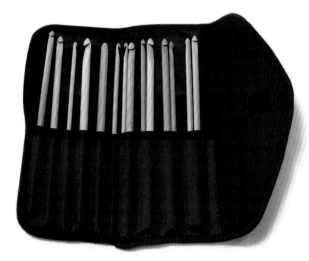

My favorite bamboo hooks.

Left Hand Tension Control

You may have a preferred technique that works for you and by all means, use it if it allows you to keep proper tension. If you are not quite satisfied with your tension, try the method I teach to my beginners. It is really easy to remember!

Your reminder is: **This is a stickup.** Position your hands as follows: Place a slip knot on your crochet hook and hold it in your right hand horizontally in front of you. (This is the bank clerk.) The right hand does not move until both hands are ready to work together. With your left hand reach out with your palm up ("give me the money") and place the working thread coming from your right hand

between the ring finger and little finger of the left hand. Close your fingers around the thread and turn your fist toward the hook, extending your pointer to the tip of the crochet hook in the right hand. ("This is a stickup.") Now lower the left pointer and wrap the working thread from the front around your finger twice (jumping across the counter to attack the clerk), and then grab the tail of the slip knot on your right-hand hook with the left middle finger and thumb (grab the loot), adjust your tension, and you are ready for the next step. Be sure to keep the left pointer straight.

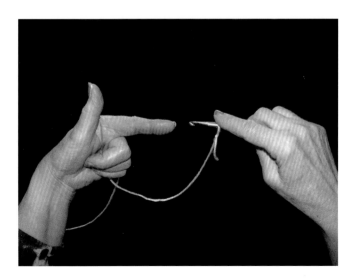

Foundation Chain

The above hand position creates a triangle, which gives you the proper place to pick up your stitches by inserting the hook with the right hand into the triangle, picking up your yarn, and pulling it toward you through the chain on the hook. Continue to chain as many times as you need to reach the desired length of your starting chain.

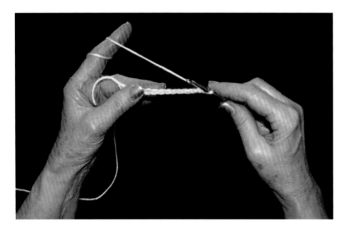

Practice

At this point, start to work your single crochet from right to left until you reach the end, chain 1 and turn. Insert your hook into the first stitch on your left, work to the end of the row, chain 1 and turn. If you have a starting chain of 15 for a skinny scarf, you will be working on 14 stitches throughout. Be sure to count your stitches at the end of each row so your project will keep even edges. This is a great challenge for many crocheters, and that's why the numbers are so important. To work in half double crochet, chain 2 and turn and your first stitch goes into the first stitch on your left and below the tiny v you see on top of your hook.

Chain 3 for double crochet, turn and skip the first stitch on your left because the chain 3 acts as the first stitch of that row. This will put your last stitch into the top of the chain 3 below. Be sure to count your stitches in each row.

Common challenges, other than tension and keeping the numbers even, are working too tight or too loose. Going up or down on your hook size as you work your test swatch often addresses that problem. Once you start with a particular hook, continue to use it—regardless of the hook's given size information. Each tool gives a different outcome and sometimes it is quite visible if you change from one hook to another, even if they are labeled the same size.

Projects for Basic Review

If you have not used your hooks in a while, it is always a good idea to review your skills before starting a new project. I usually do a quick review with a returning student, much like doing a check-up to make sure all systems are working at top performance, and to catch any challenges before they turn into a problem later.

To keep from getting bored when refreshing your basics, why not make some potholders in one of the three basics? The example shown uses Lily Peaches and Creme cotton. Starting on a 26–28 foundation chain (depending on the size you like), continue to work in single, half double or double crochet until you reach the square or rectangular shape you want, ending with a chain 10 for a hanger. Then simply slip stitch into the stitch next to the base of the chain, cut your thread about 2" away from the hook, and pull tight to secure. Now use your big eye needle to secure that tail. Be sure to guide the needle into the material before inserting the tail into the eye. This way you can see where the needle (and therefore your tail) will be travelling and you can make sure it stays invisible. Also give it a little slack so it can travel easily.

For potholders, placemats, or anything around the kitchen or a BBQ grill, always use 100% cotton. If cotton gets too close to the fire it will singe and go out. Acrylic will create flames.

Another fun basic project with the Peaches and Creme cotton is to create square baby washcloths, starting with 22–24 foundation chains. I love making the color choices and usually use three different shades of blue or pink, create a square, and roll it up like a cigar. Put three together with a pretty ribbon, and presto—Baby Bottom Bundles!

BROOMSTICK LACE

knitting needle or an actual broomstick. Traditionally a broomstick was used, but the modern variant is a plastic, wood, or metal knitting needle or smooth wooden dowel. A larger needle or dowel will result in a lacier effect, while a smaller one will provide a more closely woven effect.

As with other forms of crochet, the base of the pattern is a chain stitch. (See complete directions in the next section.) We start with our foundation chain and then pick up loops around the broomstick. After the broomstick is filled with the desired number of loops, you can work them off by putting 3 single crochet in 3 loops (or 2 in 2 loops of something fuzzy, like mohair). As long as the number of stitches and chains combined remains the same, your project will stay flat and retain its shape.

Broomstick lace is sometimes called jiffy lace in old pattern sources, I guess because it does move along quite fast. I have seen it called peacock stitch as well. Regardless, it is easy and lots of fun! I usually teach broomstick lace as a first lace technique after students master the basics.

Although there's not much historical evidence about broomstick lace, it probably originated in Europe. Americans claim broomstick crochet as their own because there is evidence that the early settlers used it as a quick way to make needed items. They are credited with this skill; as we know, even when resting, women had to keep their hands busy! By working any available yarn, threads, or even strips of cotton from worn clothing around the end of a broomstick, they formed loops and worked them into "eyes" as time allowed. Products of these early efforts were blankets and rugs.

In America, Canada, and Australia, broomstick lace is still practiced as a traditional craft and often demonstrated in rural life museums.

Nowadays broomstick lace combines the use of a crochet hook and another long, slender item, such as a

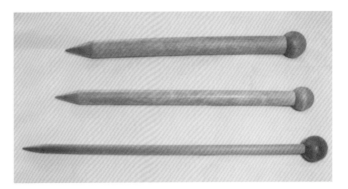

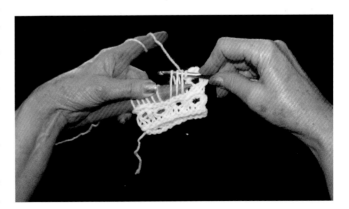

After forming the eyes, in the next row you can continue to pick up loops for more of the same or work a row or more of half doubles, doubles, or whatever suits your fancy. You can change back to the broomstick technique at any time by picking up your loops again in the next row.

Many years ago the broomstick was traditionally held under the left armpit to work the pick-up row. I find that very difficult to do for any length of time and prop my broomstick between my thighs to do the pick-up motion. This gives me two free hands and supports the broomstick on the chair below.

Here you can see my technique, which gives just the right resistance to make the job easier. In this picture I am working the pick-ups from the foundation chain. It's easy when you have both hands free!

I work a lot of baby designs so I started using size 15 and 19 knitting needles for them to keep little fingers from getting caught in the larger eyes. I use the same technique with these smaller needles as I do with the size 50 knitting needle. Try your hand at different size knitting needles.

Be sure to adjust the size of your yarn and hook to the size of the needle; I love to use bedspread cotton or fine baby yarn with the size 15 and 19 needles.

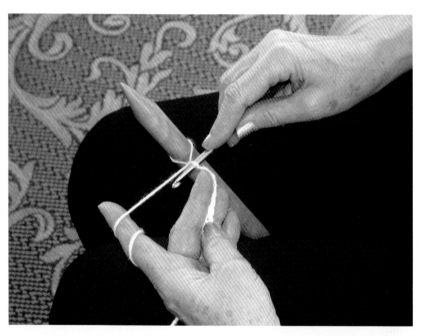

Let's work a swatch:

Supplies

    Smooth broomstick or size 50 knitting needle
    Desired yarn and appropriate crochet hook

Let's begin:

The number of beginning stitches are in multiples from 3 to 6, depending on the desired effect and the size of your yarn or thread. The first row can be done immediately in broomstick lace or in single or half-double crochet stitches. The "broomstick" is then used in the next row as one loop is picked up through each of the stitches in row one or from the foundation chain and transferred from the hook to the stick. You may wish to work a chain one at the bottom of the loops before pulling them over the broomstick to stabilize the base row if you like. Once the loops have been pulled up, turn your project, put the tip of your broomstick and your hook nose to nose, slide the hook into the loops and work them back off the broomstick by sliding them onto your hook in groupings from 3 to 6 loops at a time and working the same amount of single crochet stitches through the top of each group of loops.

Let's practice:

Chain 16, pull the last loop over the broomstick, position your broomstick between your thighs, resting the bottom on your chair to get the needed resistance. Now put your hook though the previous chain on the left, yarn over, pull yarn through to a long loop and slip over the broomstick. Keep some tension on that foundation chain with your left hand. Continue in that manner until all loops have been pulled through the chain stitches and put over the broomstick. Now release the broomstick from your leg hold and position it vertically in your left hand, nose to nose with your hook in the right hand. Then slip the hook into the first 4 loops, slide them off the needle, yarn over and pull through those 4 loops. Now work 4 single crochet into that "eye." Continue with the next 4 loops, etc., until you have four "eyes." Turn, pull the last chain up and over the broomstick, repeat the process.

Some interesting possibilities for pattern variations:

When working the loops off your broomstick, try working 4 half double or 4 double crochet into each group of four instead of putting 4 single crochet into each group. When doing this, remember to chain 2 or 3 before working the first group to get the needed stitch heights. You can place chain stitches between the groups if you like, just keep your numbers even to keep your work straight.

Another variation is to separate the "eye" rows with single or half-double crochet rows to create a firmer texture.

You can also vary your basic pattern by working only 2 single crochet (or half double or double crochet) into the first 2 loops and then continuing with the eyes of 4. This will offset the pattern row for another interesting variation.

Of course you can treat any completed row of "eyes" as a base row for one of those variations or another technique altogether. The possibilities are endless.

HT Original
Canary Crib Cover
Italian baby acrylic
Here you see the pink and blue rows worked over a size 50 knitting needle (closest in diameter to a real broomstick) and the three rows in between worked over a size 35 knitting needle in the same technique.

After completing the piece I picked up loops around the edges over the size 35 needle to give it a perfect border and finished with a picot trim.

HT Original
Sea Foam Baby Jacket
Italian cotton
Here I used a size 19 knitting needle as a broomstick and added two rows of half double crochet between the eye rows. I repeated one eye row on the front trim by picking up the loops after the two half double crochet rows down the center and completed the jacket with a shell and picot edging.

HT Original
Detail of the Sea Foam Baby Jacket

HT Original
Snowflake Broomstick Set
Here I used British virgin wool with tiny beads woven in. I worked the yarn over a size 15 knitting needle with single and half double rows in between. The buttons I purchased in Finland; they are made from reindeer horn.
There was just enough yarn left to create a cute elfin hat to complete the ensemble.

Another fun idea:

HT Original
A Princess in Stitches Jacket
Italian baby acrylic
If you are a knitter, you can start your broomstick lace insert by knitting the next row onto a medium or large broomstick from the size you are using in your established piece. Then work your broomstick lace rows as desired and when ready to switch back, pull your stitches over your regular knitting needle instead of the broomstick to continue in your established pattern.

HT Original
Detail view of the Princess in Stitches combination jacket with chain and slip stitch trim in embroidery silk.

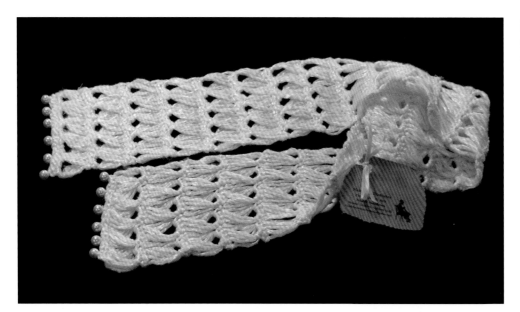

HT Original
Italian silk ribbon bridal scarf
with pearl trim

HT Original
Biltmore Flowers and Bruge Lace
Mercerized cotton
Cotton and lace liner
This christening gown in the Biltmore tradition of European style
is created from the bottom up in Bruge lace, broomstick lace, and
a French floral pattern. The hem incorporates a wide border of
Bruge lace in a graceful spiral and is trimmed with picots. The
broomstick lace rows repeat on the upper part of the sleeves. The
look is completed with twisted ties for the waist and sleeve hems.

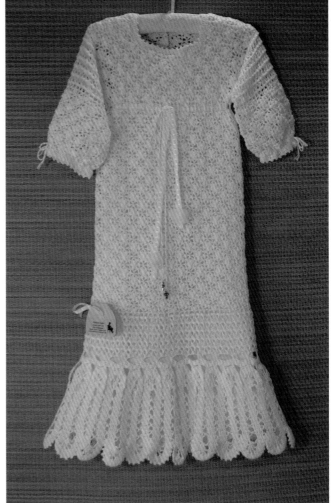

Here you can see how I picked up broomstick loops from the Bruge
hem, worked 6 rows of broomstick lace, and then switched to a
floral lace stitch, working upward to the underarm.
I repeated the 6 broomstick rows on the sleeve, just for fun!

Broomstick Mesh

If you do not wish to create eyes with your loops you can single crochet into each individual loop to create a mesh-like texture. This can be done over any size broomstick as well.

I used this same technique on my Galactic Blessings Broomstick Mesh and Star Stitch christening gown. You can see how well the bedspread cotton lends itself to this lovely pattern variation.

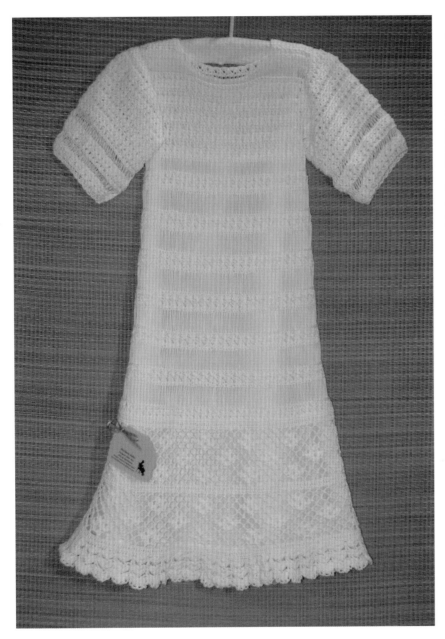

HT Original
Galactic Blessings Christening Gown
Mercerized cotton
Cotton liner

This close-up shows the broomstick mesh repeat on the sleeves of the gown. I used a size 35 knitting needle in the sleeves and a size 50 in the body.

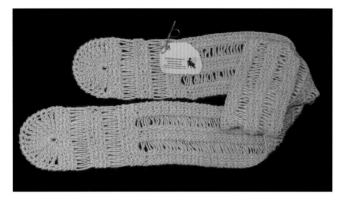

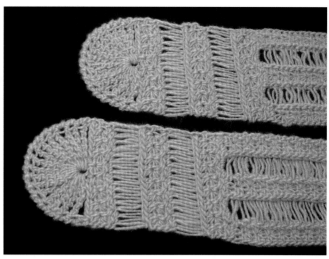

HT Original
Enchanted Afternoon Broomstick Mesh and Star stitch scarf
Italian silk and alpaca blend
Here I created a base of star stitches in my desired length for the scarf. Then I worked the mesh-like texture by picking up loops over the broomstick and working them off by putting one single crochet into each loop. I continued in the star stitch pattern for 2 rows before going back to the mesh pattern. This is done vertically in the body of the scarf and I repeated that pattern sequence on the ends horizontally and finished with a giant clam shell.

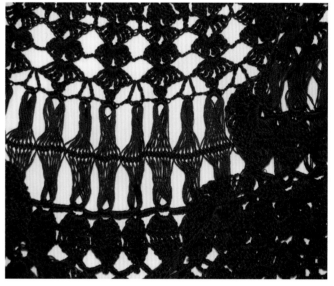

HT Original
A Mid-Summer Night's Dream
Black embroidery silk
My Mid-Summer Night's Dream Broomstick/Hairpin Combo Wrap was the first piece that inspired me to combine hairpin and broomstick lace techniques. From the hairpin strip foundation it was easy to pick up the hairpin eyes over the broomstick and continue from there. I just switched to another tool. I also interspersed crochet shells and diamonds to create a tapered shape with a swing hem. The finishing touches are a pair of tassel ties and a tassel which graces the center back neckline. Broomstick lace and hairpin lace really complement each other!

Detail view of Mid-Summer Night's Dream

HAIRPIN LACE

The traditional form of crochet known as hairpin lace was historically known as fork work, and is also known as Maltese crochet. Folklore in the British Isles tells of little girls using their mothers' hairpins, which ranged from small pins of gold and silver to larger ones of bone, ivory, and tortoiseshell. These provided an assortment of widths needed to create interesting strips. The earliest documentation of hairpin lace is found in the British Isles. Some say it was used in the court of Queen Victoria; she had many lovely hairpins to hold her mantillas when attending mass. The technique was later practiced in Malta, maybe due to the fact that it was a British possession.

Much later the hairpins were replaced by metal U-shaped tools called forks. Later these sturdy forks were available in the US in several different widths; now commercial hairpins are made to adjust to those widths all in one tool.

I personally prefer to work on the old metal forks with wooden cross bars. If you find them at garage sales or antique shops, snap them up! They are easier to work with, especially when removing the completed strip, and they hold hundreds of loops for long projects.

Hairpin lace is formed by wrapping yarn around the prongs of the hairpin to form loops, which are held together by a row of crochet stitches worked in the center, called the spine. Creating the strips is like baking the cake; it is the basic foundation of your work. The fun comes when you decide what to do with your strip or strips—that is, how to frost and decorate your cake. Much more on that later.

I prop my hairpin against my stomach when working to give the movement some needed resistance. That also makes it easier to push the completed loops toward the bottom cross bar when you work on a long strip. When working a very long strip, sometimes your bottom cross bar wants to come off, so I often use the needle stoppers that knitters use to keep the yarn from sliding off their needles; one on each prong will do the trick. If your strip needs to be extremely long and no more loops will fit onto your fork, you can remove the stoppers and cross bar and carefully slide most of your strip onto your lap. You can roll or fold the removed strip and place it in a plastic sandwich bag to keep it even and clean. Then you can continue putting more loops onto your hairpin until the desired length. The drawback of this method is that you need to carefully turn your attached work or bag each time you turn your hairpin. I always try to keep all of my desired

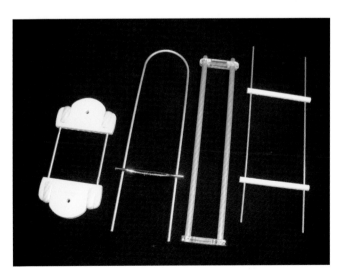

Pictured tools from left to right: Modern hairpin, antique metal pin, antique wooden hairpin, adjustable pin.

loops on the hairpin until I reach the length I need for my project. Unless you use very heavy yarn you can put several hundred loops on each side.

That brings us to the topic of counting. If you are creating a one-strip scarf, don't worry about it. If you need the same number of loops in several strips to match your work, count the loops on each side and then count again. It is almost impossible to undo or add to your strip because the constant twist in one direction as you create the spine in your work gives you a macramé-like knotted texture.

The finished length of a strip is similar to the length of a foundation chain worked in the material you are using. It is hard to gauge the length after you start to work on the fork because the loops are pushed together, so you might want to do a chain count to establish the number of loops before starting a particular project.

To make counting along the sides of the fork easier, I place a small safety pin after loop 50, 100, or whatever number is useful, just in case I lose count. It is easier to go back several loops instead of several hundred. The pin will just fall out when you remove your strip later on.

If all this makes your head spin, let's look at the easy part. Here are my basic instructions to get you started.

Practice

Supplies
> 2" or 3" hairpin lace loom
> Desired yarn and appropriate crochet hook

Let's begin:
To start, make a slip knot and place on the left prong, adjust it to position the knot between the prongs in the center. Hold the fork in your left hand and the hook in your right hand. Bring yarn around the right prong from front to back. Insert hook between the 2 strands of loop on the left prong. Yarn over and pull through, chain 1. Move hook to the back between the rods by turning it slightly to allow it to move to the back of the fork. Turn the hairpin clockwise ½ turn, (like turning the pages of a book) this wraps the yarn around the prong and you are ready to single crochet into the loop on your left, again—between the 2 strands. Sometimes I slide the tip of my left thumb nail into the loop to facilitate this motion.

Continue until your desired length, count if needed, then remove the cross bar and carefully slip your loops off the hairpin; do not cut your thread! Chain 5 or 6 chains from the top center and pivot your work counter clockwise to your left. Now you can crochet the loops together in groups of anywhere between 3 and 9 loops with the corresponding number of single crochet in that group of loops (3–9) to keep strip flat.

Try to vary this process by using just one or two single crochets in the eyes of the loops and compensate with chains in between to keep the strips flat.

You can work your strips to any length you like, then remove the cross bar of the hairpin and slip the loops off the end. Once the strip is released from the cross bars it has a tendency to curl dramatically, which was the novelty of the popular fluffy scarves from a few years ago. To keep the spine flat I slide it off the hairpin with one hand gently on top of the strip as a guide. Then I let the strip slide onto my lap before proceeding with the chains on the top. Now it is easier to work along the sides.

Depending on your planned project, you can use pretty much any kind of thread or yarn to do this; hairpin lace has unlimited possibilities!

One Strip Wonder
Think about using just one strip in a beautiful thread or yarn, give it a nice border and finish for a dramatic statement. If you choose to continue to work on that single strip, remember not to cut your thread when your loops are completed so you can work the needed number of chains to reach the first set of loops on your left. Now you can create the border, often very similar to the broomstick technique because the loops invite us to create eyes along the edge of the strip.

A single strip can be used as a scarf, shoulder strap, or as a hem. For a fun garment hem, slide the correct number of loops off the hairpin, finish the left side of the strip by chaining 5 to the loops, then put 4 or 5 single crochet into 4 or 5 loops to the end of the strip, chain 5 again to slip stich into the bottom center spine to secure. Then—get the scissors and cut the opposite loops open for the fringe. Don't fear, the spine will keep your project intact. Now you can work from the bottom up into the established loops in any desired pattern to complete your project.

On the opposite end of the spectrum I have used very fluffy mohair with just two loops per eye. As long as you adjust your hook to the yarn or thread and the number of loops to your eye, your work will stay smooth and flat. See the similarity to broomstick lace?

The fun starts when we use a little math to make things interesting: For a wavy appearance you can use embroidery cotton to loop 9 together with 4 chains in front of the eye, 1 single crochet into the eye and 4 chains behind the eye. On the opposite side of the spine you can now work three groups of 3 to complete the group—just be sure to have the same number of loops on your hairpin on each side of the fork—I am not too fond of adding loops or taking strips apart after the fact. Figuring the mathematical possibilities, once inspired, is lots of fun!

The Strip Joint

If you are working on a piece where several strips will be connected, it helps to count the loops on both sides of the hairpin and place a small safety pin every 50 or 100 loops to be certain of the correct count. Recount before sliding the strips off the hairpin to avoid any surprises later on. Hairpin lace strips behave similar to macramé in that they are very hard to undo or add to once you finish your strip.

HT Original
One Strip Wonder
Mercerized embroidery cotton
Here I worked one strip into a sash for a wedding dress; there are also matching shoulder straps with giant clamshell ends. Using mercerized embroidery cotton, I made 4 loop eyes with beads inserted along the sides and tassels for a nice finish.

HT Original
Loops of Sunshine Vest
Italian acrylic

Putting It Together

Most often the strips are crochet together. Start by working a row of chain stitches over the eyes on each strip (like chain 3, skip 3 sc below–the eye–sc, then chain 3 again and so on). Then to put two strips together: chain 3, sc into the corresponding chain loop on the second strip, chain 3, back to the first strip, sc into the loop and so on until you have completed the connecting row.

You can also use a shell stitch with a chain in the center and connect your strips by alternating the chains in the adjoining shells.

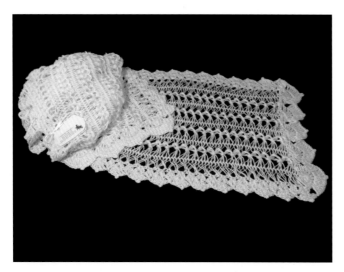

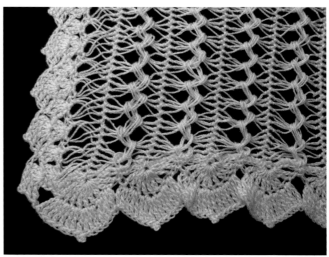

HT Original
My Buttercup Love Wrap is created by weaving five hairpin strips together and finishing with picot edged clam shells all around.

Buttercup Love edge detail

Of course, you don't have to put several strips together in the conventional way. You can pick up your loops and work them like broomstick eyes, you can then switch over to the large or small broomstick technique. Or you can even slide them onto knitting needles to start knitting. On the opposite side of the strip are more possibilities for fun, so why not just cut the loops and create a fringe hem while working up on the other side?

More Possibilities

1. You can join adjacent strips by laying them side by side. Use a crochet hook to draw up the first loop on the right side through the same loop on the left side, then pick up the next loop on the left and pull it through the next loop on the right side. Continue to alternate sides until all loops are worked. Secure the last loop to the center of the strip. See how nice it is to have the same number of loops on all strips?

2. I often use two strips, finish one on the left side and one on the right side (just turn them, you will always work to the left), align them next to each other with the open loops

nearly touching. This works well on a table or even your lap. Now weave the free loops in groups of 3 or 4 (same as your corresponding eyes on the outside of the strip) together. Use a large hook to get all 3 or 4 loops on the hook, start on the left and pull them through 3 or 4 loops on your right, then pull the same number on the left, then right and so on. Secure your last group of loops in the direction it lays with a short piece of matching yarn. This makes a beautiful braid effect and requires no yarn or thread to complete. So if you run short on material, this is the way to go.

Another Great Design Idea

If you want to insert a single strip of hairpin lace between two pieces of fabric, you can finish each looped edge by working a single crochet through 2 loops and a chain 1, repeat to the end and work the opposite edge to match. You can even use these narrow loops as a guide for embroidery stitches!

Creative Design

When designing wearable art with hairpin strips, measure front to back across the shoulders, this will be your longest piece. Then add another strip of the same length to get the width of the shoulders, another (shorter) for the underarm. Then add one or two center back strips and two front strips to create the neckline you want. Match the other side to this design and there you are! I always have a notepad handy to record the number of loops used for each piece, which you can establish once you have your shoulder strip by counting the loops to the heights you want to create,

then accurately work your strips to match the strips on the opposite side.

For the Loops of Sunshine vest I made my strips as follows: shoulders first, underarm, 2 center back and 2 front strips. I crochet the strips together as described in "Putting It Together" above. This will give you a bit more width in the body and you can make garments fit any body style and size.

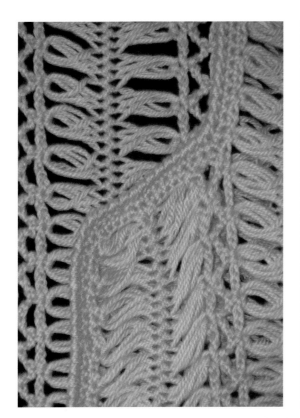
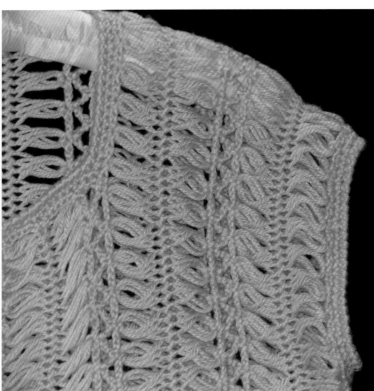

Detail of hairpin strips connections and shoulder detail. Here all the hairpin strips are crocheted together to allow for fitting adjustments.

HT Original
How Green is the Ocean Baby Sweater made from nubby
Italian cotton. All hairpin strips are woven together, long across
the shoulders and shorter corresponding strips for back,
underarms, and sleeves.

Detail of How Green Is the Ocean sweater
with twist ties. Reverse single crochet gives
a polished finish to all edges.

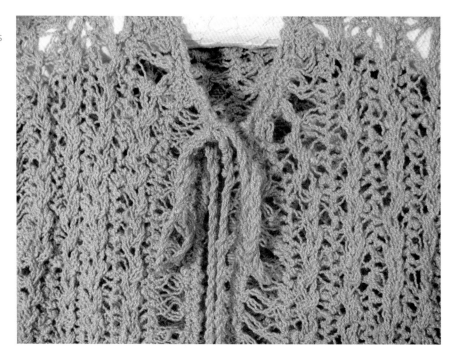

Hairpin Cluster Lace

Another interesting hairpin lace variation is the cluster stitch instead of the single crochet spine in the center. It will space your outer loops further apart but creates a very interesting center strip.

Have your first loop ready. Then, instead of going between the loop on your left with your hook, place your hook on the left under both loops and do a yarn over and pick up thread three times. You now have 7 loops on your hook. Yarn over and pull through all 7 loops on the hook. Slip stitch to secure. Now push your hook to the back of the fork and turn like the pages of a book. Then repeat the cluster on your left until your work is as long as desired. Once you pull this strip off the fork, chain 5 or more to reach the first loop on the left, then single crochet 2 or 3 times into each loop to keep your work flat. In my sample here I edged with a crab stitch, which is a reverse single crochet.

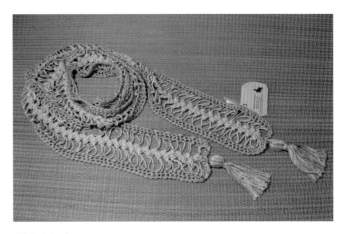

HT Original
Ocean Waves and Clusters Hairpin Scarf
French cotton and silk blend, cotton tassels

Here you can see the interesting cluster spine.

Hairpin Lace in the Round

You can also use a hairpin to create round objects, such as doilies. It is fun to gather all the loops on one side of the fork very tightly and letting the loops on the opposite side fan out in a circle. Then secure the center, connect the spine and create a fancy outer edge or connect another strip to this center strip by careful calculation of working 2, 3 or more loops for each loop you want to meet on the outside of the center strip. One circular strip can form the center of a christening bonnet or bridal headpiece.

Hairpin Lace as Trim

Another use of a very narrow hairpin (try ½" or 1"), size 30 or smaller thread, and a #13 or 14 steel hook, is the creation of fancy trim, maybe for handkerchiefs. After you work the desired length, remove your strip from the fork and create a smooth edge on one side of the strip as follows: Chain to the first loop on your left, now put 2 single crochets into each loop, taking care not to twist your strip. I keep it flat by laying most of the strip on my thigh before picking up the stitches. Then do another row of single or half double crochet on that side to create a nice base to attach the edging to your piece.

On the opposite edge you can create shells, picots, bullions, or whatever you like. Sometimes I put a base row of 2 single crochet into each loop on this edging side as well to create a base for any fancy shells, etc.

Block your edging by pinning and wetting the thread; let air dry before sewing to your garment or hankie from the wrong side. Then carefully steam your finished project very lightly under a cotton cloth.

HT Original
Merry Go Round Doily
Mercerized cotton
Here I completed the first round with a fancy shell design but kept on going and established the needed number of loops to connect a second strip with larger eyes and the same fancy shell finish around the outside.

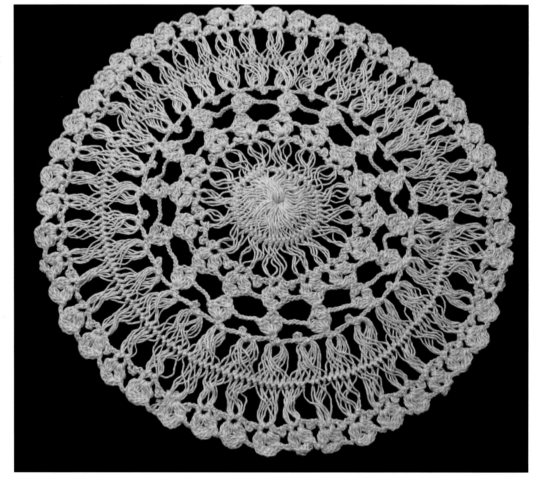

Hairpin and Broomstick Lace Combinations

Another design idea is to create baby carriage covers or bed covers by combining broomstick and hairpin lace in delicate materials with a fancy border.

Hairpin lace is so versatile and just begs to be combined with broomstick lace or any other possible techniques. Just working the strips will inspire you!

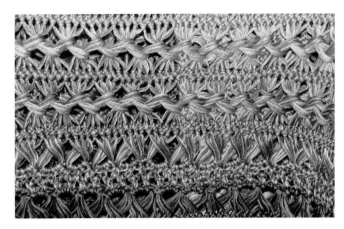

HT Original
Appalachian Sunset Wrap

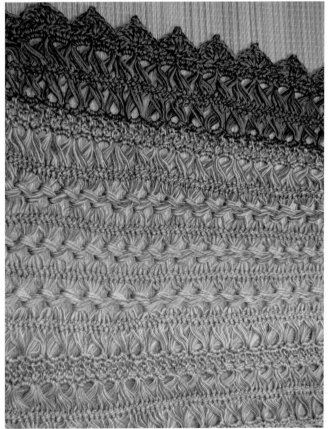

Hairpin/Broomstick Lace Combo Close Up
Here loops and spines from the hairpin strips intermingle with lengths of broomstick lace. Some of the hairpin strips are finger-woven together, others are crochet together in this particular piece. I used several strands of American Super Luster Pearle cotton for a nice blend of colors.

HT Original
Royal Baby Heritage Bed Cover
American baby acrylic

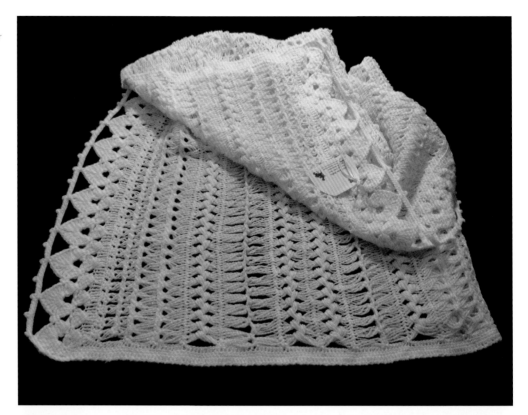

Here you can see the hairpin
strips woven together on one
side, and then I turned the
piece to pick up loops over a
size 35 needle for broomstick
lace; in the next row I worked
the broomstick lace over a size
19 needle. To finish the piece I
changed from fingering yarn in
the hairpin/broomstick sections
to soft acrylic in the same pale
rainbow shades to provide a
stable edge for this piece.

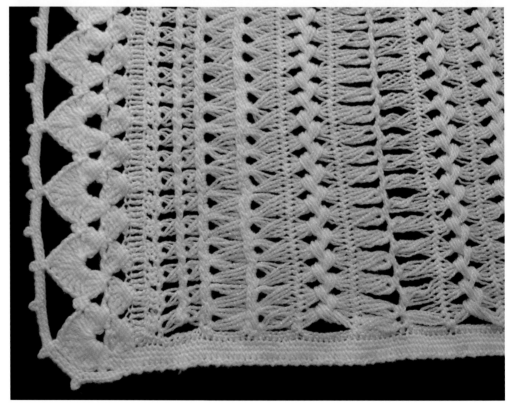

TUNISIAN CROCHET AND LACE

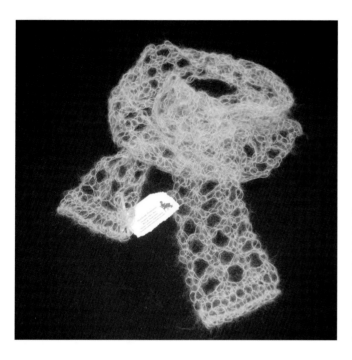

Tunisian crochet has somewhat of a nomadic past and the stitches appeared under many different names over the years, Afghan crochet being one of the most popular ones. Based on my research I believe that Tunisian crochet originated somewhere in central Asia ("Afghan" after all comes from "Afghanistan") and moved west through the Middle East (with a stop in Tunisia) and up into Europe and Scandinavia. The actual name "Tunisian crochet" is credited to the French, maybe because France occupied Tunisia for a while.

Patterns appeared in the early 1800s and were called Afghan stitch, Tricot crochet, Scotch knitting, Railroad knitting, and Hook knitting, plus a few more regional names. The most enduring ones are Tunisian crochet and Afghan stitch, with Tricot crochet a close third.

After the early patterns in the 1800s, Tunisian crochet appeared in publications less frequently, and by the end of the nineteenth century it was close to unknown. Then it was seen occasionally in the 1930s before it faded away again. The 1960s and '70s saw a revival, and Tunisian crochet enjoyed another resurgence in the late 1980s.

Originally it was a popular technique for blankets, afghans, and other solid-textured items. It soon fell out of favor because of its tendency to roll and be unyielding. However, I always liked the idea of the forward and reverse pass without having to turn my work. I really fell in love with it once I started to play with the technique on much larger hooks, like the N, P, or Q hook. Used with a textured material, such as mohair or narrow ribbon, it creates a very interesting look.

Tunisian crochet is often mistaken for knitted work because it has a similar look. Included here are directions for a Tunisian simple stitch, Tunisian double crochet, Tunisian Cross stitch, and the Afghan knit stitch. Once you have tried these, go on to the Tunisian lace.

For most Tunisian crochet stitch techniques you start with a chain of the desired length and then the process continues with a forward pass of picking up a loop through each chain. Without turning, the loops are worked off in a reverse pass with either a simple pull-through stitch, or some lacy variations, which are beautiful on any edge. The Tunisian lace is my personal favorite.

Tunisian Simple Stitch

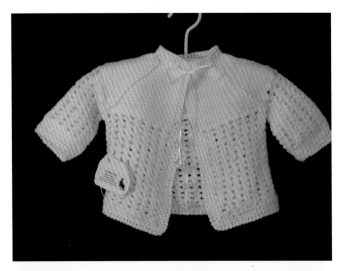

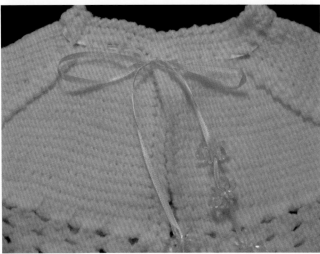

HT Original
Tunisian Dreams Baby Jacket
Tunisian simple stitch bodice
Worked in baby acrylic on K afghan hook.
This is the stitch most of us are familiar with. If worked with K hook or smaller, it has a tendency to roll up. This is why I believe the technique fell out of favor a few years ago.
Try this same Tunisian simple stitch technique with a larger hook and some full bodied material, such as mohair or ribbon.

Tunisian Crochet

Supplies:
Hook and yarn

Basic Instructions

Start with a chain of desired length and then the project continues in a forward and a reverse pass. After the base chain is worked, insert hook into the 2nd chain from hook, yarn over, draw loop through and leave the loop on the hook. Insert hook into the next chain and repeat until end of chain. Do not turn. This is the forward pass.

To work loops off the hook, do a reverse pass as follows: yarn over and draw through one loop only. After this first stitch, continue with yarn over, draw through 2 loops; continue to yarn over and draw through 2 loops until one stitch remains on the hook. You have now created a row of vertical bars. Do not turn.

From here you can continue with a Tunisian Simple Stitch:

Your next forward pass begins with that remaining single loop on your hook. Skip the first vertical bar in the row below, insert hook into next vertical bar, and yarn over. Draw a loop through and leave it on the hook. Work loosely! Repeat until one vertical bar remains, work this last stitch through the front vertical bar only. Do not turn!

On the reverse pass, yarn over and draw through one loop only, after the first stitch, do a yarn over and draw through 2 loops, until one stitch remains. The row of Tunisian Simple Stitch is completed.

Tunisian Cross Stitch:

A nice variation of the Tunisian Simple stitch is to cross over your first and second vertical bar, draw up the loop from the third vertical bar below and leave on your hook. Then cross back over to the right and draw up your loop from the skipped vertical bar. Continue to skip one vertical bar, pick up and then cross over to pick up your loop. This creates a nice X pattern.

Another fun variation you can do is the Tunisian Double Crochet (tdc):

Tunisian double crochet is worked through the front vertical bar of the previous row. The forward pass begins with the single loop on the hook. In order to accommodate the height of a row of tdc, chain 2. Skip the first vertical bar, yarn over, insert hook from right to left behind the next vertical bar and yarn over, pull through 2 loops only, and leave the last loop on the hook. Repeat until one vertical bar remains.

The reverse pass is always the same in Tunisian crochet: Yarn over, draw through one loop only, continue with yarn over, and draw through 2 loops until one stitch remains on the hook.

The Tunisian Knit Stitch:

I love this variation because it really does look like knitting. With a regular hook this stitch makes your work very dense and less stretchy, so it is a good choice for sweaters and other warm pieces. If you want a lacy knit effect, choose a large hook and material with a bit of body, like a soft mohair.

Start with your regular foundation row as before. Now insert your hook in the second chain from hook, yarn over, pull up a loop and leave on the hook, insert hook in the next chain, yarn over, pull up a loop, leaving it on the hook. Repeat this stitch to the end. There should be one loop for every chain. Do not turn your work.

For your return pass chain 1, yarn over, draw through one loop only, continue with yarn over and draw through 2 loops until one stitch remains on the hook.

The next row is the knit forward pass: Skip the first vertical bar, insert hook between the strands of the next vertical bars (under the horizontal strands), yarn over, pull up a loop, leaving it on the hook. Again, be sure to work loosely! Repeat this stitch to the end. There should be one loop for each stitch. Do not turn.

Now work your return pass, then repeat the forward and reverse passes for the length of your project.

For another variation you can also work your forward pass stitches directly between the upper horizontal strands, just be consistent to retain the pattern.

Midnight Lace Tunisian Wrap

HT Originals
Left to right: Tunisian half double crochet with Roman Circles (see the "Finishing Touches" chapter).
The knotted scarf in the center is made from soft mohair on a P hook.
The Italian ribbon scarf on the right is made in simple Tunisian crochet.

HT Original
My Midnight Lace Tunisian Wrap
Alpaca blend

Tunisian Lace Stitch

Make a base chain with a number of loops you can divide by four.

After the forward pass of picking up all loops, do your reverse pass as follows:

Yarn over, draw through one loop, yarn over and draw through 2 loops on hook, chain 4, yarn over and draw through 5 loops on hook (cluster made), chain 4, yarn over and draw through 5 loops on hook, repeat to end and finish the row with yarn over and draw through 3 loops on hook.

For the forward pass chain 1, skip the first of the chains, insert hook in the next chain, yarn over and draw through the next loop 3 times, skip over the next cluster, insert hook in next chain, yarn over, draw through one loop in each of the next 4 chains, repeat to the end.

Repeat the above two rows to the desired length and finish off with 2 rows of single crochet worked between the vertical bars.

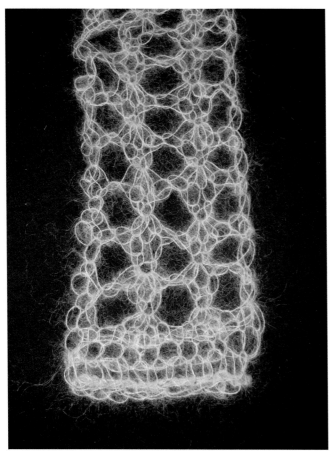

Hints

This lovely variation is lacy when used to make a shawl, and it is beautiful as a border.

There are several companies which make bigger hooks with extensions for your larger pieces to accommodate any number of chains. I use a Denise interchangeable hook, size 19 or Q.

You can finish any of your Tunisian projects with one or more rows of regular crochet, half double or double crochet stitches, worked between the vertical bars. Picots or other trim can be added from here. This keeps your piece from curling.

Tunisian simple and double crochet work tends to curl, and one way to control this is to use a large hook and work your base row and bind offs loosely. Don't hesitate to block your work by pinning, moistening, and air drying. You can also edge with standard crochet stitches.

A fun combination for you knitters is to slide a knitting needle from the right side of your work through the loops before starting the reverse pass. Then you can turn your work and actually knit any pattern you like from here on. Your yarn will be in the correct place to continue to work, but beware, you will be on the wrong side of your project.

As you can see, Tunisian crochet lends itself to lots of possibilities. What fun to revive this old-fashioned technique!

THREAD CROCHET

Thread crochet encompasses any technique you can work with fine thread and small hooks. We will take a closer look at Bruge lace, bullions, limpets, filet crochet, and Irish crochet in this chapter. However, you are never limited to those techniques, as any stitch or pattern you like can be worked in thread crochet. I used a ladies jacket pattern to create a baby sweater in embroidery silk. The reduction was just perfect! You can use the broomstick technique over a smaller (size 15 or 19) knitting needle in a baby project or use your hairpin fork and bedspread cotton (or smaller) to create delicate edgings or inserts. I use all of those combinations in my christening gowns and Victorian baby items.

Thread crochet is one of my top favorites. I love making pretty borders around handkerchiefs for bridesmaids'

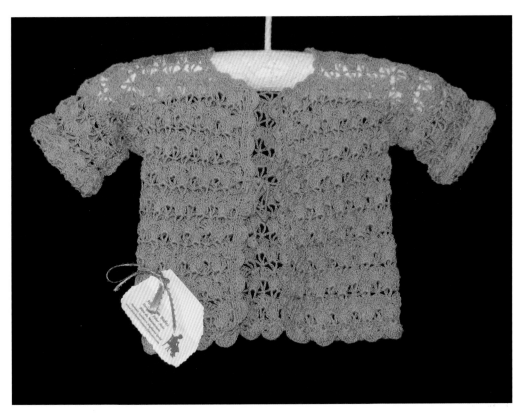

HT Original
A Rosy Celebration baby sweater, inspired by a ladies' jacket ca. 1940
Soft Italian cotton
I added the shell trim around the edges and clam shell ties for a cute finish.

Here you can see the one-piece construction, which is worked from the bottom up. There are only shoulder seams, and the sleeves are worked into the armhole. Detailed directions are in the "Be Your Own Designer" chapter.

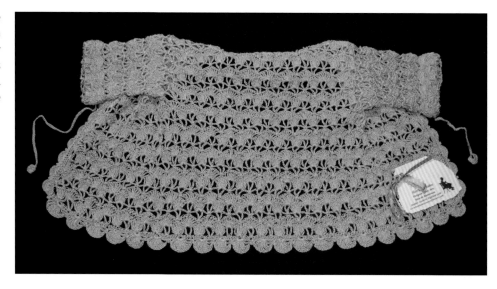

gifts in colors to match the gowns or fold them in half and gather the fold side to create a baby bonnet as an heirloom gift. My christening gowns are usually worked in thread lace and upward from an interesting hem. Then the design develops and the gown tells me how to proceed and when to switch to another stitch or technique.

Thread crochet is fun and doilies are a great way to start. Why not use a vintage pattern for a very small one to make a set of six interesting coasters? They don't have to be white or ecru, in fact, bold colors look very contemporary and you can match them to your décor.

Spiral Project: Doll House Rug or Coasters

Supplies:

Cotton/silk twist and 0 hook

or

#10 bedspread cotton and size 7 hook

Directions: Chain 4, join with slip stitch to form ring.

Round 1: Chain 1, work 8 sc in ring, place marker and work in continuous rows from now on.

Round 2: Work 2 sc in each sc around (16 sc). Move marker.

Round 3: Sc in next sc, 2 sc in next sc (24 sc). Repeat to marker, move marker.

Round 4: Sc in next 2 sc, 2 sc in next sc. Repeat around (32 sc).

Round 5: Work 2 sc in next sc, sc in next 3 sc, repeat around (40 sc).

Round 6: Sc in next 4, 2 sc in next sc, repeat around (48 sc).

Round 7: Sc in each sc around for border. (48 sc).

Of course you can work in rows by slip stitching into the top of your first stitch once you come around. Chain 1, 2, or more to get the desired heights for your next row of stitches and continue on the right side of your project, or chain and turn. This way you can work a front and back appearance of your pattern. The number formula on the increase stays the same, two in each stitch on the second row; then two stitches and then one in the third row, and two stitches and one stitch twice in the fourth row and so on.

From here you can graduate to simple or more complicated doilies. There are thousands of doily patterns available in print and on the Internet so I only want to give you an idea of something interesting to do with such a pattern.

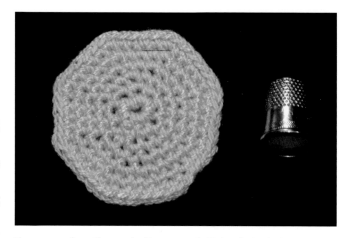

You can see how the gradual increase of stitches helps to keep your round piece flat. This works for any size project, from these coasters to a room size rug. This is a miniature for a Victorian dollhouse.

34

More Design Ideas

Another common use for thread lace is the lace border for pretty hankies. I have edged many bridesmaids' hankies with beautiful colors to match their dresses and although thoroughly old fashioned, this is still a great gift.

On that same idea I love to use white, rose, or pale blue to edge a hanky and turn it into a baby bonnet to be given to the newborn and to be kept until their wedding to be used as something old or something blue for the bride.

As you can see, the applications for thread lace are endless. Let your imagination and some old books or magazines inspire you!

HT Original
Hospitality Cake Cover
Mercerized cotton
This cake cover was inspired by a doily pattern. I made the original foundation chain loop large enough to go over the glass knob and then shaped the rest of the cover to adhere to the glass dome by decreasing the number of stitches given in the directions to keep the doily flat. Just play with it!
To complete the look I added silver charms to the tips in the bottom row.

BRUGE LACE

HT Original
Detail of the Bruge lace hem on Belgian Flower Garden vest
This piece is worked in fine Italian cotton and finished with
matching covered buttons, featured in the "Finishing Touches"
chapter.

Sometimes spelled with two *g*'s, Bruge lace is also called
Brussels or Battenberg lace in some of my old books
and magazines.

Trips to Belgium as a little girl introduced me to the
local bobbin lace, worked with several bobbins secured
to a velvet pillow with metal pins. Intricate patterns have
been handed down for centuries and the crochet versions
have been documented for about 200 years. This crochet
version was originally developed to imitate the much more
expensive bobbin lace worked in Bruge and surrounding
areas. Working with a multitude of wooden bobbins required
training and years of experience, so the crochet version
soon became quite popular. Traditionally crochet Bruge
lace is worked in fine white cotton or linen thread; I have
used the technique as the hem on one of my christening
gowns but also use it freely in more colorful pieces.

Here is a basic pattern for Bruge lace. (My pattern
was inspired by one in *Crocheting School,* a book that's
now out of print, but offers an excellent starting point for
design creativity.)

Chain 10, dc in seventh chain from hook, dc in each
of the remaining 3 chains = 4 dc made. Chain 6 and turn.

Work dc into each dc, chain 6 and turn work. Repeat
to desired length to make a simple strip to use as trim.

To make the serpentine as seen in the pictures, work
10 rows as before, then begin the curve as follows:

Next row: Dc in 2 dc, half double crochet in next dc,
sc in last dc, chain 6, turn.

Following row: Sc into sc, hdc into hdc, dc into 2 dc,
chain 6, turn.

Repeat these last 2 rows twice more.

Next row: Dc in the first 2 dc, hdc in hdc, sc in sc,
chain 3, then insert hook through the three chain 6 arches
worked after sc and do a slip stitch to draw them together.
Chain 3 and turn.

Sc in sc, hdc in hdc, dc in 2 dc (curve is complete),
chain 6 and turn.

2 dc, hdc, sc, chain 3.

Yarn over and draw up a loop in the slip stitch that
was made to draw the arches together, yarn over, and draw
through 2 loops but do not complete the dc. Insert the hook
into the next free arch and draw up a loop, then in one
motion draw it through to join the free arch and complete
the dc. Chain 3 and turn.

*Dc in next 4 dc, chain 6, turn your work, dc in 4 dc,
chain 3, slip stitch into the next free arch to join. Chain 3,
turn work.*

Repeat step 8 (* to *) three more times, then work the
curve as before, from step 1 to 5 in the serpentine sequence.
Join your new straight section to the existing section as
in step 6. Continue in this manner for desired length.

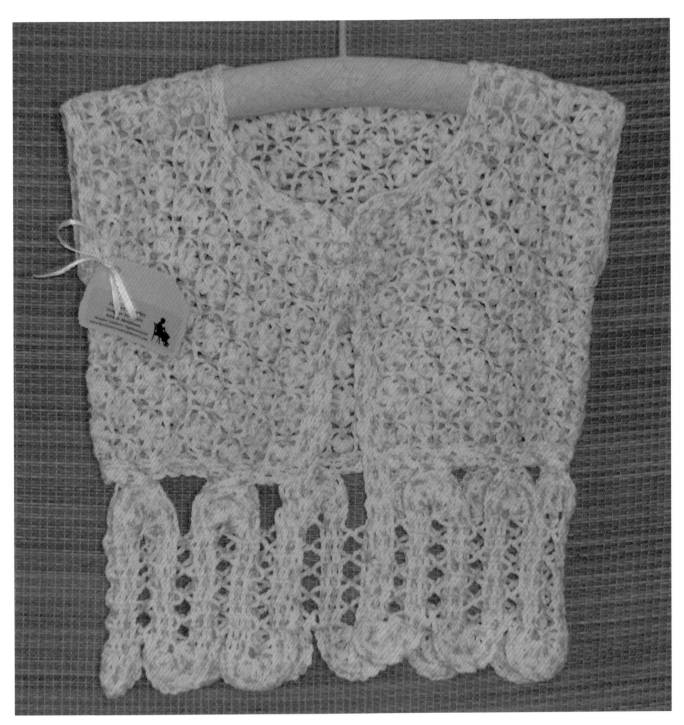

I love using this serpentine as a hem for many delicate items. The pattern works for yarn as well, but I prefer to use bedspread or other thin cotton thread to feature the beauty of the serpentine. After you finish the desired length for your hem or border, turn your work and crochet across the top of the serpentines with as many chains as needed to get to the top of the next one. This will enable you to work upward in any desired pattern for the rest of your piece.

Here is another Bruge lace hem on a baby sweater:

HT Original
My Aran Little Boy Blue
sweater with Bruge lace
hem and limpet stitch trim
Mercerized cotton

HT Original
Here is the hem on my
Biltmore Flowers and Bruge
Lace Christening Gown.
Mercerized cotton

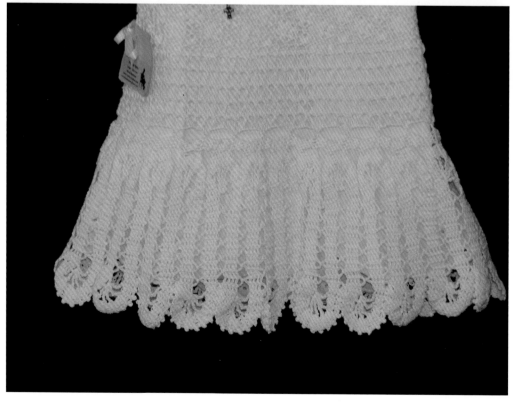

BULLIONS AND LIMPETS

History tells us that the bullion stitch is traced back to elaborate garments of the Roman Empire.

The coil technique of ancient embroidery designs was adapted to crochet, creating the interesting rolled texture. Bullion stitch is the most challenging to master and requires practice and patience but is well worth your time. There is an easy way to master the bullion by starting with just two yarn-overs and then increasing, one yarn over at a time, until you reach the desired length of the roll, up to 18-20 yarn overs with very fine thread.

Thanks to Jean Leinhauser, a well-known crochet teacher and designer, for these practice diagrams, which were published on the "Talking Crochet" website in July of 2010. Jean was a crochet legend; she passed away in June of 2011.

Bullion Practice Piece

Row 1: Ch 9, sc in 2nd ch from hook and in each ch across, turn.
Row 2: Ch 2, hdc in first st, then work Bullion st as follows:

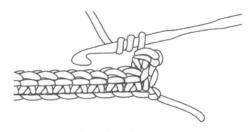

Illustration 1: Yo hook twice (be sure to wrap the yarn over the shank of the hook, not over the tapered throat).

Illustration 2: Insert hook in next sc; draw up a lp to length of a sc.

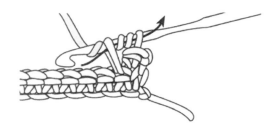

Illustration 3: Yo and draw through all lps on hook.

That basically is a short bullion stitch. Now let's make it more challenging.

In Illustration 1, yarn over hook 3 times, complete as before. Now try Illustration 1 with 4, 5, 6 or more yarn overs. You'll see that the more times you wrap the yarn over the hook, the taller the stitch will be (Illustration 4).

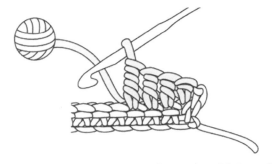

Although the Bullion stitch can be made with just about any size or type of yarn or hook, it looks best done with a crisp thread such as crochet cotton. Softer yarns give a looser, not quite as tight, coil which is still attractive.

Practice

Now let's practice with a larger swatch:

Chain 21, single crochet into second chain from hook and in each chain across. You now have 20 single crochet, chain 2 and turn. Proceed as before, but increase the number of yarn overs as you get more comfortable.

After practicing with more than 6 yarn overs on regular yarn, you are ready to use thinner yarn and a smaller hook to practice the same motion. Once you are comfortable with this, try switching to #10 bedspread cotton and work up to 20 yarn overs in one stitch. It is like growing little worms by wrapping your thread around a very small hook many times and then pulling the working thread through that tube of loops. Be sure to keep your hook facing down and try to grab the loops with the left hand and wiggling along as the hook slides through them. Try using a hook with a straight shaft; it makes the job easier than using a hook with a throat indentation. Each bullion requires a few attempts; the more loops the harder it is, but the result is well worth it.

Working an individual bullion in each stitch creates a beautiful trim. Or you can create bullion shells by putting 5 into the same stitch and then skipping 2 or 3 stitches,

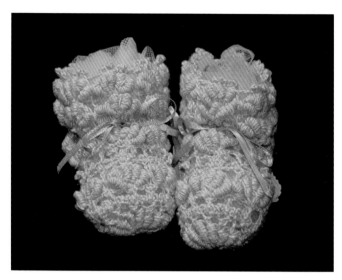

HT Original
Bullion Baby Booties
Mercerized cotton

HT Original
A Star is Born Jacket
Mercerized cotton
Here is another use of bullions as trim. This ecru thread lace jacket features a shell and bullion trim all around, as well as my clam shell trim on the ties.

single crochet, skip 2 or 3 stitches again and repeat the bullion shell. This will give you a luxurious look, as seen in the Bullion Baby Booties above.

The Limpet Stitch

You can get a similar look as the bullion with a bit less work and frustration. It is called the limpet stitch and looks much the same as the bullion, except that before putting each yarn over on your hook you twist it, much like a knitting cast on. The difference is that you do this onto a crochet hook instead of a knitting needle. Put as many stitches as desired onto the hook.

Then put your hook through the next stitch, yarn over, and pull through the fabric and all loops on the hook except two. Yarn over and pull through the last two loops to lock in the stitch. The front will be smooth with a chain down one side and the back will have a long thread going from bottom to top.

HT Original
Close-up of the limpet stitch trim on the bottom edge of this Bruge lace hem.

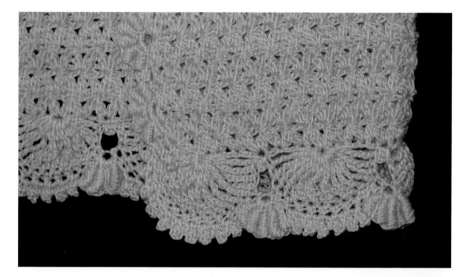

Hem and sleeve details on a Star is Born jacket.

FILET CROCHET

My Filet Crochet Pillow.

Filet crochet roots go back to fifteenth-century Italy and France, and might have been inspired by fishing nets. In fact, *filet* is the French word for "net." It is worked in a grid pattern of open and filled squares, called blocks and spaces. Filet crochet became popular around 1850. It easily replicates needle lace and, because it stays flat, makes designs and letters stand out. Bedspread cotton is the usual material but the technique can be worked in any material you like for your project. Using only two simple stitches, the chain and the double crochet, this technique lends itself to creating pictures and letters with those stitches. Like Irish crochet, it was originally done in white to signify purity, maybe because it was taught by nuns and incorporated religious designs. Cotton is naturally white as well, and dying was expensive and labor intensive.

Filet is usually worked from a chart instead of following a written pattern. The technique is quite easy but there aren't too many possibilities to get creative, so I still own my one and only piece that I worked from a chart; I take it to every show and workshop just to make a statement. You could make up your own chart and create a personalized design.

The first row of each chart is read from right to left (front), the second row from left to right (back). Continue by alternating with each row.

A good way to learn filet crochet is to start the foundation chain and basic stitches with thicker thread or yarn and a larger hook than normally used. Since only chains and double crochet are involved, you usually move right along. After one or two rows on a practice piece you could alternate one block, one space, etc., and then several blocks and several spaces. Once you get the concept of blocks and spaces, it is easy and fun to try working from charts. Then you can really see how the design develops. To make things easier, you can enlarge a simple pattern on poster board or copy on paper.

It is important to keep track of the rows, maybe with a magnetic board and attached ruler or a metal clip. Remember, rows are read from right to left on the right side rows and then left to right on the back rows.

Classic filet crochet is worked from a chart, but there are also filet patterns that can be done as a pattern repeat, such as this Filet Blossoms Festival. This was originally

HT Original
Filet Blossoms Festival Jacket
with picot edging
Mercerized cotton

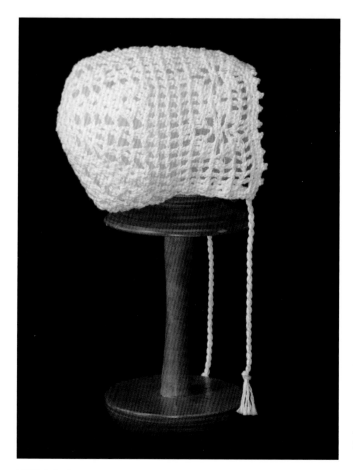

HT Original
Mercerized cotton
Matching filet crochet band on the Blossoms Festival hat.

available as a narrow trim pattern. I incorporated the flower pattern repeat in the jacket and hat.

Hints

Proper tension is really important when working with the finer thread. It is a good idea to be familiar with or have some practice with thread crochet projects before starting the filet work. Of course you can work filet patterns in heavier thread or yarn but the effect is not as delicate and clear as with your cotton thread. Once comfortable with the mesh concept, you can switch to finer thread and a smaller hook.

Your turning chains on the mesh patterns need attention, as well as watching the number of stitches on multiple blocks. A magnified chart might also be helpful, along with detailed explanation on how the pattern develops.

If you like a structured, row by row pattern, filet crochet is for you. Many patterns give you instructions on how to do lettering and other designs, which make filet pieces popular for specific applications, such as pillows, chair covers, and curtains.

Try slip stitch or single crochet with an added touch, such as the picots in my bookmark. Once finished, a larger piece of filet work may require an outside edge to give it body and prevent stretching.

Here is my quick and pretty filet favorite:

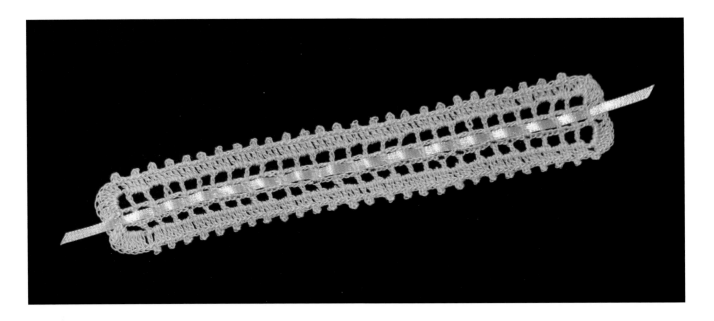

My Dainty Filet Mesh Bookmark
(No chart needed)

This works in size #10 or #20 bedspread cotton or cotton embroidery floss, but I do like the very tiny #30 thread for this project.

Materials:
   #30 Coats and Clarks cotton, #11 steel hook

Directions: Chain 89

Row 1) Dc in 8th. ch from hook, ch 2, skip 2 ch, dc, repeat (ch 2, skip 2 ch, dc) to the last 2 chains, ch 5, slip st in last ch. Chain 5, turn = 28 ch 2 spaces.

Row 2) Dc in 1st. ch of foundation row, opposite the last dc of row 1 (ch 2, skip 2 ch, dc) across the bottom of the foundation chain to the end of the row, last dc into 3rd. ch below. Chain 5, turn.

Row 3) Dc in next dc, (ch 2, skip 2 ch, dc) to last space, dc in 3rd ch of ch 5 below. Chain 3, turn.

Row 4) 2 dc in ch 2 space, dc in dc, picot, (2 dc in next space, dc in dc, picot) to last sp, 7 dc in corner space, dc in next dc, chain 2 for center row space, dc in next dc, 7 dc in corner space, dc in dc, picot, (2 dc in next space, dc in dc, picot) to last space, work 7 dc in corner space, dc in next dc, ch 2 for center row space, dc in next dc, 3 dc in beginning space, slip st to beg ch 3. Fasten off.

Insert ribbon through center row spaces.

I gave this a very light blocking by using a warm iron over a damp cloth on the wrong side of the bookmark after pinning the bookmark down in several places.

It is always a good idea to secure the corners with rust free straight pins before blocking. Larger pieces need to be pinned on a gridded cardboard cutting board; then I spray the entire project with distilled or filtered water and let it air dry. Summer days on the porch are the perfect time for this!

IRISH CROCHET AND LACE

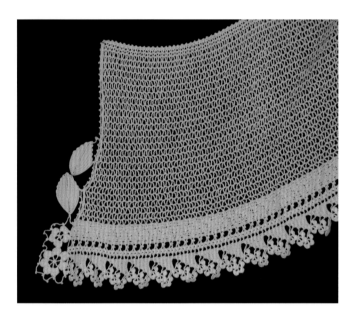

By far the most popular and best known thread lace comes to us from Ireland.

The origin of Irish lace is obscure and has been attributed to India, Persia, and medieval Italy. Historians trace most of our lace techniques back to the Middle East when fishermen made nets by tying individual knots and designs into open squares. This may be the origin of many thread lace techniques, from filet crochet to Irish crochet.

In Ireland it became known as early as 1743 when the Royal Dublin Society first awarded prizes for Irish crochet. In 1835 the nuns of County Cork were already creating unique lace designs; however, Irish crochet as we know it became recognized worldwide during the days of the Irish potato famine from 1845 to 1851. To survive, many women went into convents to learn the technique from the nuns. Other European countries were already known for their colorful designs, so the Irish ladies decided to recreate fine lace work unique to their own regions. In 1847, one of the harshest years of the famine, several teachers started a thriving cottage industry in Clones, in the northern county of Monaghan. In the same year a school for lace crochet was founded in Cork, located in southern Ireland. Using the finest threads and very small hooks, they created individual motifs like shamrocks, roses, flowers, and leaves. They were arranged and then joined with a crochet mesh fabric. Traditionally Irish crochet is worked in white but occasionally in black for mourning.

While attending high school in Germany I had the good fortune to be an exchange student in Belfast, Northern Ireland. In addition to the academic classes we received a nice dose of culture and I especially fell in love with Irish linen and Irish crochet. I enjoyed hearing about the sanctity of the local patterns, such as the Rose of Sharon, the Rose of Killarney, and the variations of leaves, shamrocks, and picots beloved in different counties of Ireland. Originally the individual motives were worked over a foundation cord to give it more body, then attached to a fabric foundation, and the background was filled in with crochet mesh.

In my Irish Flower Garden piece I created the mesh background first and then attached the flowers and leaves to the back of the wrap and the wrists. Here the flowers and leaves are created from six strand embroidery silk—it is similar to the #10 mercerized cotton but gives great choices in color shading and seems lighter and softer to the touch.

Here are some suggested background patterns for Irish lace. These can be used to connect or support floral pieces like my Irish Flower Garden or on their own, as in my Irish Christening Gown body (with picots) or the bodies of my bridal wear collection pieces.

A V stitch into a V stitch in the row below, such as in my bridal shawl, makes a nice body if you want to feature a shamrock or floral border. Picots and shamrocks inserted in the base fabric add interest. Here is a simple way to add picots:

Make a chain with multiples of seven, plus 2.

Sc into second chain from hook, chain 2, chain 4 or 5 more, slip stitch into 4th or 5th stitch from hook (picot), chain 3, make picot as before, chain 2, skip 6 chains, sc in the next chain. Repeat across, chain 6, and turn.

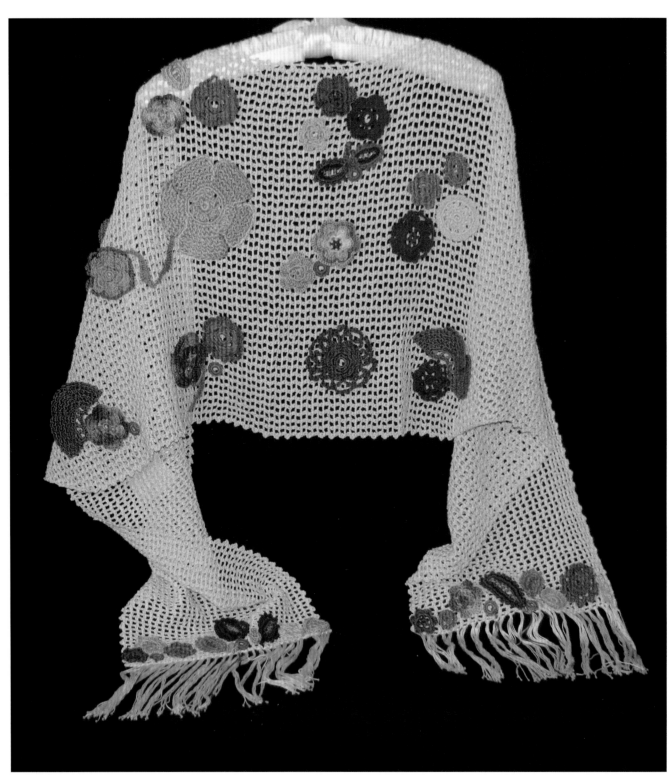

HT Original
My Irish Flower Garden
Mercerized cotton base, embroidery silk flowers

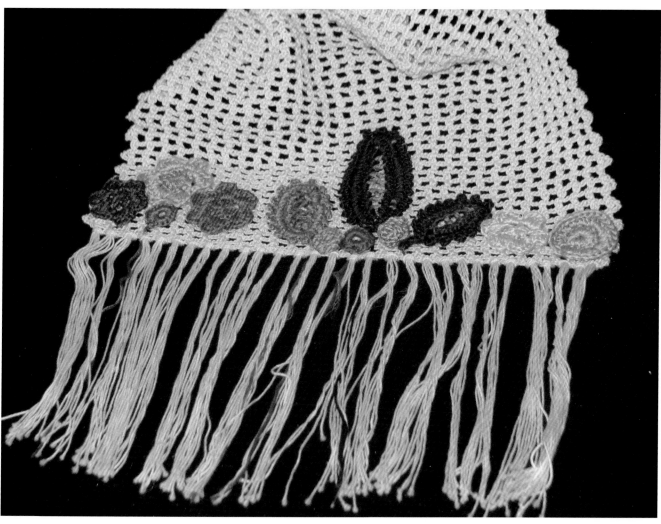

Floral and leaf details on Irish Flower Garden.

Work picot, chain 2, sc between the 2 picots, chain 2, picot, chain 3, picot, chain 2, chain 2, sc between the 2 picots, repeat to the end of row, end with a triple in the last sc. Chain 1 and turn.

Sc over the next chain, *chain 2, picot, chain 3, picot, chain 2, sc between the 2 picots*, repeat to the end of the row, ending by skip 1 chain after the last picot, sc into the next chain. Chain 6 and turn.

Repeat rows 3 and 4 until desired length.

I love Irish crochet because of the freedom of creating the flowers and shamrocks to decorate a classic or contemporary piece of work. That work can be free flowing and only your imagination limits you to design and color. Irish crochet uses lots of picots as well, and I love that combination, as seen in the Irish Rose christening gown. The bulk of the skirt features picot mesh, which is a typical Irish crochet background or base fabric. The Rose of Sharon on the chest signifies love and life, and the blossoms on the shoulders represent the guardian angels protecting the child. The hem features four leaf clovers all around, smoothing the way through the child's entire life span. The six clovers on the waist ribbon protect the internal organs. So, much significance is worked into this gown.

Sharing the Rose of Sharon Flower

With size 10 white bedspread cotton and a size 7 steel hook chain 6, join with a slip stitch to make a ring. Chain 1 and put 10 single crochet into the ring, slip stitch to join.

Chain 6 (this is the first double crochet and chain 3) skip the next single crochet, double crochet in next single crochet, chain 3, skip next single crochet, double crochet in next single crochet. Chain 3, skip one and dc three more

HT Original
Rose of Sharon Irish Christening Gown
Mercerized cotton
Cotton liner

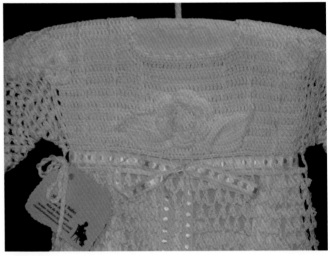

The Rose of Sharon detail.

times, chain 3 and slip stitch into the third chain of the starting chain. You now have six double crochet legs.

Slip stitch into the first chain loop, put 1 single crochet, 1 half double, 5 double 1 half double, and 1 single crochet into the chain loop. Repeat in each chain 3 loop around and join. You should have six petals.

Chain 2, back post single crochet around the double crochet post of round 2 below, chain 5, and working behind the pedals on row 2, place back post single crochet around the next double crochet, repeat around, and join.

Slip stitch into chain 5 loop, put 1 single, 1 half double, 7 double, 1 half double, and 1 single crochet in each chain 5 loop around.

Chain 2, back post single crochet around the single crochet post below, chain 7, back post single crochet around the next single crochet post below, chain 7, repeat around and join.

Slip stitch into chain 7 loop, put 1 single, 1 half double, 9 double, 1 half double, 1 single crochet into the loop. Repeat around and join. Fasten off, leaving long tail to attach.

This is the original Rose of Sharon pattern I was given in Dublin more than fifty years ago and it is still my favorite.

There is also a Rose of Tralee, Rose of Erin, Rose of Galway, Rose of Killarney, Rose of Shannon, and floral designs particular to the areas of County Clare, Londonderry, Cork, and many more. One could spend a lifetime researching and producing all the beautiful patterns that are still around.

A Leaf Pattern to Accompany Your Rose

1) Cut an 18" length of your mercerized cotton to use as a foundation cord. With a size 9 steel hook chain 15, lay the foundation cord along that foundation chain, and working over the foundation cord throughout the pattern, single crochet into the second chain from hook, single crochet in the next 12 chains, 5 single crochet in the last chain. Now working on the opposite side of starting chain, single crochet in the next 13 chains, then working over foundation cord only, 3 single crochet over the cord to form the tip. Now working down the first side again and still working over the cord, single crochet in the back loops of the next 12 single crochet, chain 1 and turn.

2) Working in the front loops only, single crochet in the next 13 single crochet, 3 single crochet in the next single crochet, single crochet in the next 12 single crochet, chain 1, and turn.

3) Working in the back loops only, single crochet in the next thirteen single crochet, three single in the next single, single crochet in the next ten single crochet, chain 1, and turn.

4) Working in the front loops only, single crochet in the next 11 single crochet, 3 single crochet in the next single, single crochet in the next 10 single crochet, chain 1, and turn.

5) Working in the back loops only, single crochet in the next 11 single crochet, slip stitch in the next single crochet, fasten off, leaving a long tail to attach. Trim the foundation cord.

One of my favorites is this shamrock border. It promises good luck to the wearer, so I often start one of my baby creations with the shamrock theme. It is worked lengthwise, and when I reach the desired hip measurement, I pivot counter clockwise and start to work upward toward the armhole.

HT Original
Clovers and Stars
Princess Jacket
Mercerized cotton

Here is another baby jacket with shamrock border and broomstick inserts.

HT Original
Royal Shamrock Jacket
Another example of
Irish crochet with
broomstick touches.
Mercerized cotton

More Projects

Another beautiful use for the shamrock blessings border is in my Bridal Wear collection. The border on this wrap is a full 72" long to reach from fingertip to fingertip before working upward toward the neckline. I shape the wrap slightly by decreasing several stitches in the last 5 rows to give a better fit around the shoulders and neck. A daisy blossom and leaf design accent the sides.

HT Original
Irish Blessing Bridal Wrap
Mercerized cotton

I created a matching hand flower to complete the ensemble.

HT Original
Irish Hand Flower
Mercerized cotton
One or two of these can be worn for a wedding or other special occasion. They were inspired by the beautiful henna body drawings that adorn brides in India.

Another example from my Bridal Collection incorporates a daisy-like flower which graces the back and hem of the Irish wrap. This piece can be worn with the border trim in the front or the back.

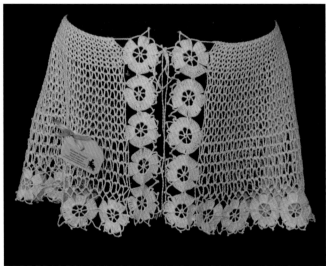

HT Original
Lucky Daisy Bridal Wrap
Mercerized cotton

More Design Ideas

I prefer to work with the customary cotton thread (#10 or #20 mercerized cotton) and # 6, 7, or 10 metal hook. Many of the original patterns of Clones lace call for size 60 or even 80 thread but I find it too small for my eyes. If you are not used to working with such small thread I suggest starting with some easy thread lace pieces and working your way toward flowers and leaves. You might also try to create a flower or leaf with a larger hook and yarn and then slowly step down to a smaller hook and thread.

Irish crochet gives the most creative freedom—any pattern suggestions are only meant as an inspiration—leaving much to the creativity and skill of the crocheter.

Last but not least, I would like to share my most precious Irish inspired piece with you. It is called Surrender to the Irish. I won third place in the 2013 "Bring Us Your Best" show, sponsored by the Henderson County Arts Council. A nice check accompanied the honors and then I was asked to donate the piece to the permanent collection of the Folk Art Center of the Southern Highland Craft Guild, which I was honored to do.

HT Original
Surrender to the Irish
Embroidery silk
This camisole combines the heritage techniques of broomstick, hairpin, Tunisian, and thread lace in the main body and moves it forward into a contemporary fashion statement by the addition of an Irish shamrock hem and traditional Irish rose blossoms and leaves. The Irish techniques take center stage here and therefore broomstick, hairpin, Tunisian, and thread lace harmoniously surrender to the Irish.

Floral details and back view of Surrender to the Irish.

ARAN CROCHET

Since I also like to knit, and I love anything Irish, I believe Aran crochet, the art of creating cables in a project, is an easier alternative to the more time consuming knitted version. Aran takes its name from the Aran Islands off the west coast of Ireland.

There is a debate about when island residents first started making cabled knitted garments. Much like the floral and leaf designs in Irish crochet, each region used a variation of cables and pattern work, supposedly to recognize any fishermen lost at sea by their garment pattern. Historians believe the designs to be of ancient Celtic and Megaliths stone carvings origin.

Some stitch patterns have a traditional interpretation, often of religious significance. The honeycomb is a symbol of the hard-working bee. The cable, an integral part of the fisherman's daily life, is said to be a wish for safety and good luck when fishing. The diamond is a wish for success, wealth, and treasure. The basket stitch represents the fisherman's basket in hopes for a plentiful catch.

Most historians agree that far from being an ancient craft, Aran knitting was invented as recently as the early 1900s by a small group of enterprising island women, with the intention of creating garments not just for their families to wear but which could be sold as a source of income. These women adapted the traditional Gansey jumper by knitting with thicker wool and modifying the construction to decrease labor and increase productivity.

Traditionally, an Aran garment is made from undyed cream-colored *báinín* (pronounced "bawneen"), a yarn made from sheep's wool. Sometimes black sheep's wool was used. The yarns were originally made with unwashed wool that still contained natural sheep lanolin, making the garment essentially water-repellent. Until the 1970s, the island women spun their own yarn on simple spinning wheels or drop spindles.

I have created a swatch for you to practice a very authentic looking cable that can be used as a center part for anything from a scarf (great for that masculine look) to the front center of a sweater. For babies and children I love to use continuous cables as in the blue Aran sweater here.

To work the Aran cables with your crochet hook, you need to be familiar with front and back post double crochet

HT Original
Little Boy Blue Sweater
British wool with tiny beads accents

(fpdc and bpdc). To do so, bring your hook around the entire front post of the next double crochet below. The hook is inserted from the front on the right side of the next post, guided around the back, and out again on the left side of the post, then do your yarn over to complete the dc. For the back post double crochet insert the hook from the back around the post in the front and then back, yarn over, and complete your bpdc. This creates the texture needed to make the cables stand out.

Be sure to work loosely so the cable can stand out without puckering. If you work tightly, go to a larger hook size on this technique.

Aran Cable Practice

Work on a base row of double crochet. In the next row start with 3 double crochet, then simply skip 3 stitches in your pattern, front post double crochet in the next 3 stitches, then cross over the three you just worked and go back to fpdc into the 3 skipped stitches (from right to left); dc in the next 2 stitches, skip 3 and repeat the fpdc pattern. End with dc in the last 3 stitches. On the next row start with 3 dc, put a back post dc in each of the next 6 stitches, then 2 dc in the double crochets below and repeat across. In the third row do your 3 dc, then front post dc in the next 6 stitches, then 2 dc, and repeat across. This creates the cable effect.

Practice Swatch

Chain 23, dc in 4th chain from hook and each chain across = 21 dc. Turn.

Row 1 (right side): ch 3 (counts as first dc), dc in next 2, skip next 3 sts, work fpdc in next 3 sts, work fpdc in each of the 3 skipped sts, dc in next 2 sts, repeat across, ending dc in last 3, turn.

Row 2: Chain 3 (for first dc), dc in next 2, bpdc in next 6 sts, dc in next 2 sts, repeat across.

Row 3: Chain 3, dc in next 2 sts, fpdc in next 6 sts, repeat across.

Row 4: Repeat row 2.

Rows 5–16: Repeat rows 1–4 three times.

This would make a lovely scarf in a wool, wool blend, or acrylic yarn.

The technique will require some patience and practice; be especially careful to pick up the 6 bpdc in row 2. Count each time to avoid any surprises on the cross-over row after you chain and turn.

After you master the swatch, try some variations: You can space the cables further apart or create just a center cable in combination with other stitches for a masculine look.

HT Original
Aran Princess cable jacket
Fine Italian cotton

Close-up of the Aran Princess cable technique.

HT Original
This cheery Summer Garden Tea
Party Topper was created from
twelve Aran rectangles, made in
nubby Italian cotton. Proper size of
the rectangles assures a perfect fit.
Minor adjustments can be made
when the pieces are connected.

Design Ideas

Aran crochet can be worked in very fine to medium thread or yarn and can be combined with other techniques. In the blue and white sweater seen below I worked the Bruge lace hem first as a strip, then, once it was long enough for the desired hip measurement, I turned the piece to work the cables in the pattern up to the underarm. Then I separated the piece into two fronts and the back and continued in this manner to the shoulder seams. The sleeves were worked directly into the armholes and feature the cable pattern as well. See more about this design technique in the "Be Your Own Designer" chapter.

As you can see, the possibilities are endless when working with Aran cables. Although it does require some practice, I know you will enjoy the results!

HT Original
The Belgian Prince Aran and Bruge lace baby sweater
It features a limpet stitch border and my clam shell trim on the ties.
Mercerized bedspread cotton

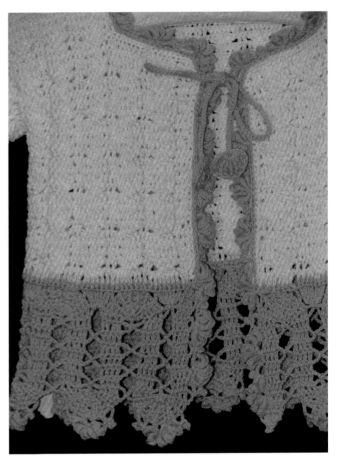

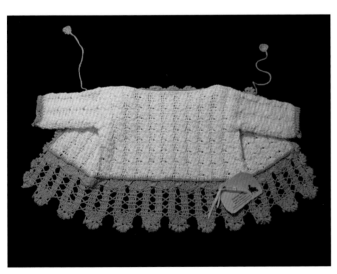

HT Original
Detail view of Belgian Prince construction from the hem up.

WORKING WITH BEADS

Growing up in the 1950s I remember seeing tiny beaded purses in many antique shops in Europe. My grandmother owned such a treasure and I recall her sadness when it fell apart one day, and she saved the tiny beads and the metal closure in a special wooden box. Unfortunately I don't know what happened to it!

The roots of bead work are obscure, but we know that it was especially popular in the United States from 1860 to 1880 when it was common to work hundreds of tiny beads into elegant evening bags. Many publications call the technique Swag Stitch. This technique resurfaced in the 1970s and is now called Flat Work. It is a more advanced technique of working with small glass beads and is for those among you who like technically precise crochet. It creates a solid bead on bead fabric as you crochet a bead into each stitch in every row. This is often worked from a

chart and limited to smaller pieces, such as decorative pins, jewelry, small purses, or brooches due to the weight of the beads. The results are beautiful! Flatwork is a very disciplined technique; if you like structured work you might give it a try. I think of it much like filet crochet—once you start with the technique you are committed and there is not much room for variations.

There are many other ways to use beads or pearls in any given piece you might be working on. I prefer to work #6–10 beads into my wearable art pieces as trim or finishing touches.

A special request to incorporate beads into a christening gown inspired me to string hundreds of tiny beads onto an interesting cotton thread to work up a beaded scarf. This was meant as practice before planning the larger piece. I found the Easy Floss Dental Threaders the best aid in picking up tiny glass beads to transfer onto my thread. After I started to work on the scarf I remembered that the beads show on the wrong side, which made for an interesting pattern in itself and is not too important on a long scarf. I also noticed the weight of the piece increased the more beads I incorporated. This really prepared me for the possibilities and pitfalls of creating a christening gown in that technique and I decided to limit the beads to the hem of the gown and trim around the neck and sleeves.

To incorporate beads into your project you need to figure the number of beads needed to do the job. I always add more beads than needed. Use the ones that glide easily through the yarn or thread as to not stress your material any more than necessary. If you use different colors, remember to load the beads in the reverse order.

For size 10 thread, as in the christening gown, use #8 or 10 beads. There are other possibilities; just use your creativity as a guide.

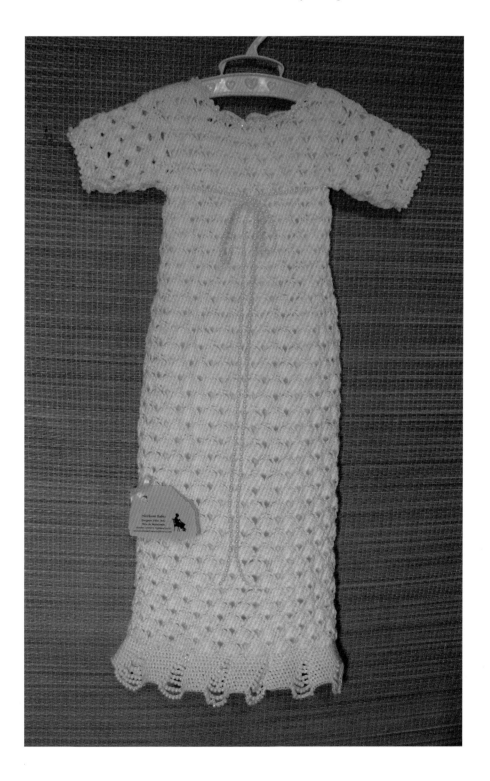

Hem of my beaded christening gown.

HT Original
Top and sleeve trim of the beaded
christening gown
Mercerized cotton
Cotton liner

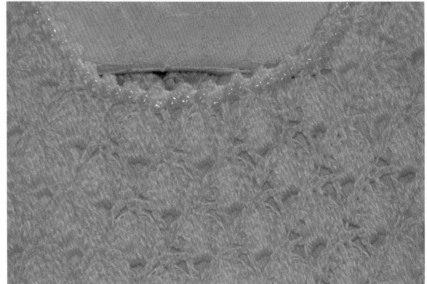

Practice

To work a bead single crochet, insert your hook into the desired stitch, slide a bead up next to your hook, yarn over and draw up a loop, yarn over and draw through both loops on the hook. This has to be done on the wrong side so your bead shows on the right side. Trim edging looks nice when you place several single crochets between your bead stitches. You can also do a half double bead crochet as follows: Yarn over and draw up a loop, slide bead up to your hook, yarn over and draw through all 3 loops to complete the stitch. Work 2 or 3 half doubles between your beaded stitches for a nice effect.

You can slide several beads to create a loop before the yarn over through both loops. This creates an interesting effect for your trim sections.

I prefer to add beads into my larger pieces in a planned fashion, as the pictures show. They also lend themselves to finishing touches on the ends of scarves or along the edge of a special piece, such as this Irish bridal wrap.

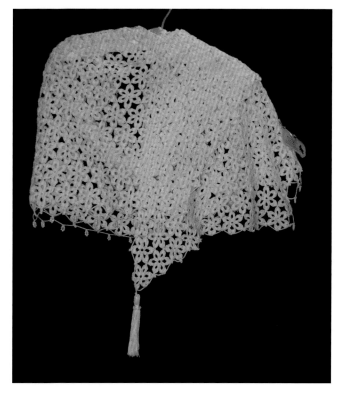

HT Original
My Irish Blossoms Bridal Wrap is trimmed in white #6 beads.
Soft Italian cotton

HT Original
Carnival in Rio scarf
Italian cotton with glass beads
This was the practice piece that inspired the hem on the
christening gown.

Hem detail on Irish Blossom Bridal Wrap.

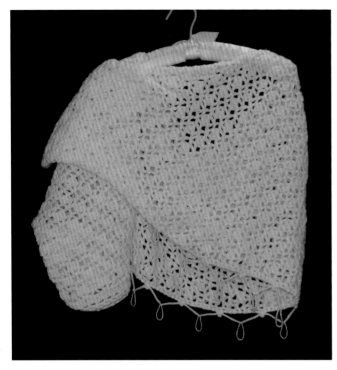

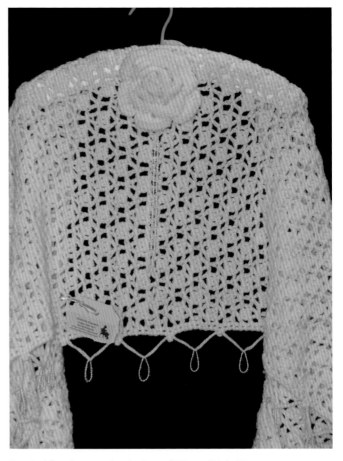

HT Original
My Winter Bride Wrap features dozens of 20-bead loops of clear
#10 glass beads
Fine British wool and alpaca

Beaded floral accent back view of Winter Bride Wrap.

Winter Bride hem detail.

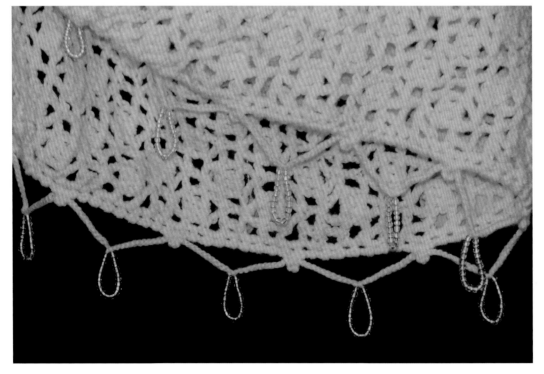

Try stringing your beads with the Easy Floss Dental Threader, work your hem base row, maybe chains and single crochets, then move as many beads as you like to where you want to create a loop. Slip stitch the loop together and continue with chain stitches in your established pattern.

I always keep an array of #6, 8, and 10 glass beads on hand for instant design ideas and gratification. They truly add a nice finish to a special project. Many projects look very rich when worked on a metal thread. Try it for a change from your cotton or silk threads.

The larger plastic beads available in many craft stores are also fun to work with, as you can see in my Maltese Splendor piece.

Beads can enhance any of your designer projects and are easily incorporated when you work on broomstick or hairpin creations.

Keep some beads close to your yarn and thread stash and they will give you ideas on how to get together!

HT Original
Maltese Splendor Hairpin/Broomstick combo
Embroidery silk with beads
Hairpin lace is sometimes called Maltese crochet, hence the name of this piece.
On this combination wrap I used the larger plastic beads in different colors, just for fun! They reflect the color variations of the embroidery silk and are placed along the hem, in the first broomstick row along the neckline, and along the sides of the wrap.

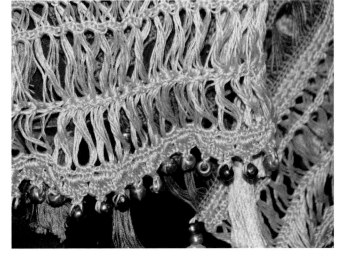

HT Original
Embroidery silk
I combined hairpin and broomstick lace techniques and alternated the colors to reflect the change of light. After starting with the hairpin strip I was inspired to start a broomstick pattern and insert beads along the top. There are more beads along the hem of the wrap. The sides feature eight beaded tassels. Finger weave and star stitch are incorporated as well.

THE FINISHING TOUCHES

An Easy Button. See the directions on page 64.

HT Originals
Left to right:
Hand spun wool in broomstick lace with a clamshell finish, thread lace scarf with picot trimmed clamshell, and alpaca Tunisian lace with broomstick and floral accents and crab stitch finish.

A personalized finishing touch makes any design piece special—it's like fancy frosting on a cake instead of plain powdered sugar!

For that special touch, try to pick up loops around the borders of a project and continue with a broomstick lace border (see How Green Is the Ocean sweater) or a Tunisian lace border. Also use the beautiful embroidery threads on the market now to create ties, tassels, and flowers, or cord edging for any fashion design to give it a Coco Chanel effect. You can use those threads for I-cords and braids as well; you can even cover buttons to match your project.

Three Options for Finishing the Short Ends on a Scarf

1) Use reverse sc (**crab stitch**) or finish with beads and pearls attached with matching sewing thread.

Do the crab stitch as follows: Working from left to right, draw up a loop in the next single crochet to the right, 2 loops on hook, yarn over, draw up a loop through both loops on hook. Continue to the end of row.

Sometimes I use a hook one size smaller than used in the project to adjust the tension.

2) Or **do a giant clam shell** of triple or double triple crochet (yarn over 2, 3 or 4 times, pull through 2 stitches at a time until back at the top), do your yarn overs again, stitch into the center of the bottom row of the project and repeat your tall stitches until the clam shell lays flat (usually 9-12 double triple crochet or more—you will be able to tell when it looks right without puckering).

3) **Also try Roman Circles:** start a long chain in the corner where the scarf or project ends and chain 60-90 tight loops (depending on the yarn) and sc the last one into the opposite end to secure. Turn and work 2 slip stitches toward the center and then chain 45-55 tight loops back to the other end, secure with a sc. Again, do 2 slip stitches toward the center and then chain 25-30 tight chains back to the opposite side. You can do this with as many or as few circles as you like.

You can edge any project with picots:

At any edge work a base row of single crochet. In the next row chain 1, single crochet in the first 2 sc, chain 3, slip stitch into the first of the chains. Single crochet in the next 3 stitches and repeat.

My grandmother slipped into the front of the first of the chain 3 and into the front of the stitch below as well before finishing with the slip stitch. This looks great and gives a bit more stability to your trim.

Fringe Instructions

With many of the beautiful new yarns available today, a fringe edging is very effective.

Use a 12" ruler to cut one or two length of yarn for each beginning chain stitch.

Put your crochet hook into the first chain from the back and pull the folded length of fringe through the stitch, put both ends through the loop created, and pull to tighten up. Finish each stitch along the bottom with a length of fringe. To trim even, I put my project on a table, line my fringes up at the edge of the table, and smooth out the ends. Then cut across with sharp scissors and catch the fall-out in a wastebasket below.

On a larger piece, such as a shawl, stole, or afghan you might cut your fringe material much longer and pull two or four lengths together through the stitch. Do not attach in each stitch, but a few inches apart by skipping the same number of stitches each time. Then take two lengths of the fringe to your left and knot with two lengths of the next fringe on the right. Progress across your project and then do a third row of knots below that. With this technique you can add beads into the fringe before you knot the two pairs together.

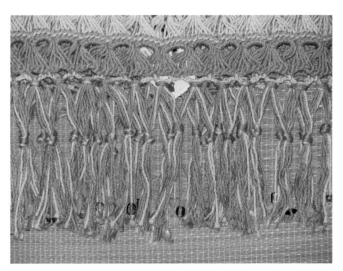

Knotted fringe with bead inserts.

Crochet Fringe

You can also do a simple crochet fringe by chaining tightly to the desired length at the end of your project, then use the same amount of chains to come back toward the next stitch and slip or single crochet into that stitch to secure. Again, chain the same amount of stitches and come back to secure in the next desired stitch. You can also return to the same stitch and slip stitch or single crochet into that one for a fuller effect before moving to the next stitch on the right or skip one or two stitches for a more "loopy" look.

You can vary the length of the fringe by using a different number of chains each time. This gives a more relaxed, casual look.

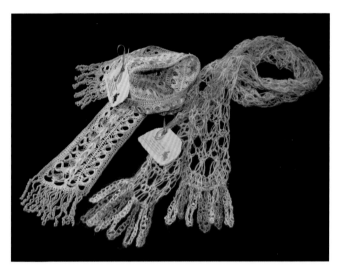

HT Original
Old fashioned bedspread cotton turns into a two-tone woven hairpin scarf with crochet fringe; Tunisian lace in soft mohair with tiny glass beads also features the crochet fringe.

Tassel Instruction

Tassels are easy to do and give a fun finish to many projects. I love to use embroidery floss for a fancy tassel and often use metallic thread for the wrap. Here we go:

Cut two 5" lengths of your wrapping material and set aside.

Wrap your tassel yarn anywhere from 20 - 40 times around four fingers (or a larger object, such as a book, cell phone, etc.), then cut the thread. Put one of the reserved lengths of thread through the loops and knot tightly. Now wrap the tassel where desired, (usually about ½" to 1" below the top knot) by using the other length of yarn or thread to create a U-shaped loop and pulling the thread through that loop and around the tassel, wrapping in the opposite direction of the flow. This gives a tight finish and keeps the wrap from coming undone. After wrapping as desired, pull the ends through the center with a large eye needle, then attach tassel as desired. Cut threads on the bottom open and trim even. Completed tassels can be trimmed with beads, charms, etc., before attaching and made any size you desire.

open end, cut your scissors free on the bottom, and secure with a tight knot.

These are nice for baby booties with a pompom trim or as ties for babies' or children's items.

HT Original
A purple wool-acrylic blend and soft Italian cotton produce more braided hairpin strips with tassel endings.

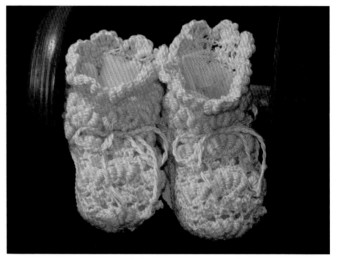

HT Original
Baby Bullion Booties with twisted cords
Mercerized cotton

Embroidery and Beads

You can also embellish your work with embroidery accents. Rows of crochet stitches can be used as a guide for cross stitch, or use floral designs or French knots through both thicknesses of your work for free flow designs.

Beads are another option for embellishment. (See the Working with Beads chapter.)

There are no limits to your design imagination here!

Easy Buttons

The easiest way to cover a button is to use one from your button box. Select a button with a shank that is smaller than the desired end result. Thread or embroidery floss works best for this, although a fine yarn will work as well.

Leaving a long tail, crochet a chain 3 or 4, slip stitch into the first chain to connect to a circle, and then work 5–8 single crochet into the center of the circle. Be sure to work over your tail in the first round and then give it a little tug to pull the center stitches together before going to round 2. Here you will need to increase, so 2 single crochet in each or every other stitch is called for. The shape of your button will guide you. A flat button needs a circular shape (2 sc into each stitch) and a domed or rounded button requires a sc increase in every other stitch. When you get

Flowers and Leaves

Don't overlook the possibilities of adding a floral theme to a hat or any other creation. Blossoms on a wrap, carriage cover, or fingerless gloves can make your piece something special. Refer to the Rose of Sharon and its leaves in the Irish crochet chapter for more inspiration. Lots of nice flower directions are available on the Internet, so go for it!

Twisted Cord

Cut your material six times the finished length of your cord. Find your center and slip over a hook or door knob. Start to twist the strands from the open end, away from you. Be sure to retain good tension to keep the twist tight. Now slide one scissor handle to the center of the twist. Remove from your hook or door knob; holding both ends, center the scissors and let them dangle at the bottom and they will create your natural twist. When it stops, knot the to the outer edge of the button top, place a single crochet in each stitch to shape the edge. Now place your button inside and decrease every third sc or so, enclosing your button until you get to the shank. Now your button is completely covered and you can fasten off and use this end and the tail end to secure your button to your project.

I love to use embroidery floss for these buttons, and I use the same color strands to trim my project or create the twisted cords to match.

My Easy Breezy Smarty Cardy is a great example for using embroidery floss to give a simple design a classy finish. It features the buttons worked over a plastic ring, and a simple ch 3, skip 2, slip stitch edging.

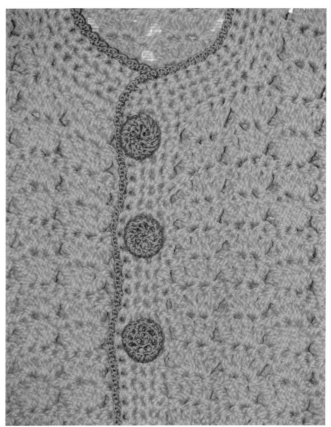

Trim and button detail in embroidery silk featured on East Breezy Smarty Cardy.

HT Original
Easy Breezy Smarty Cardy
Wool and alpaca blend

There is another way to make buttons using a plastic ring:

Using the embroidery floss, work 30 single crochet over a ¾" plastic ring.

Row 1) Chain 3, 2 dc tog (dc decrease) around the ring, slip stitch to top of ch 3, fold toward the middle, ch 1.

Row 2) Work 2 single crochet tog (sc decrease) to fill the center, fasten off, and pull thread to the inside.

Row 3) On the outside, run a length of thread through the 30 sc, pull the start and end of the thread tight and knot, fasten off. Leave tails to sew the button to your project.

HT Original
Mercerized cotton with metallic thread
This 3" by 4" Gold Rush Treasure bag features buttons worked over a plastic ring. It was made for the 2014 "It's a Small World" exhibition at the Folk Art Center on the Blue Ridge Parkway in Asheville, North Carolina.

Blocking

A final word about the most important finishing touch: Blocking. I block most of my finished pieces by pinning them onto a cardboard cutting board with grids, using rust free pins at every inch or even closer, using the grid lines as a guide. Spray your piece with a fine mist of filtered water and let air dry before removing the pins. You will be pleased with the results!

Both cotton and acrylic fiber benefit from blocking this way. Please do not use a hot iron!

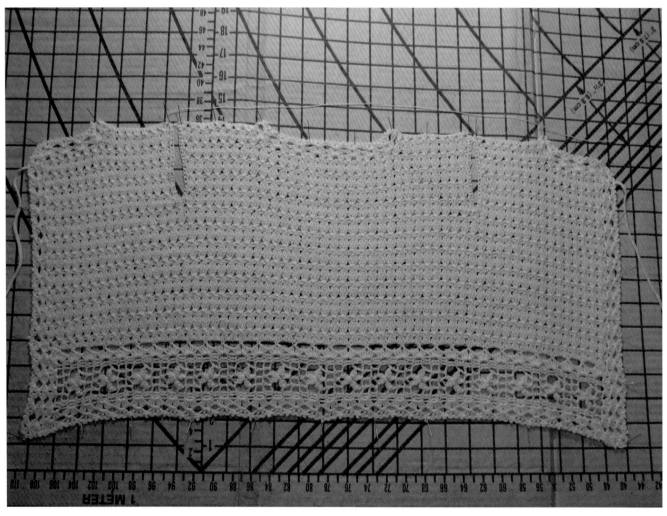

HT Original
A baptism jacket in the making
#10 American bedspread cotton

BE YOUR OWN DESIGNER

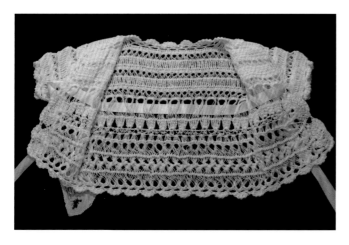

Going into a yarn shop or down the aisle of a craft store, you can't help but get ideas! The beautiful colors and novelty yarns invite you to be creative, and it is fun to think of a project that will be your very own creation.

When you pick a skein of yarn in a favorite color, be certain to check the label—not only to get an idea of the care instructions, but also the amount of yarn in your skein. Thicker yarn has a shorter running length. I always suggest buying extra and keeping your receipt. Or, if you really like what you are buying, just plan on putting any extra material in your stash.

Now we come to the challenge of using a pattern. If you have patterns you like, by all means, go for it. Vary small details or the trim to develop your independence and personal style! That is a nice first step. I also suggest using a tried and proven adult pattern to create a baby or child's sweater or hat just by using a finer yarn and a much smaller hook. The same can work in reverse—if you love a child's pattern, use bulkier yarn and a larger hook for an adult version.

By now you probably have some favorite stitches and techniques. So use them in one of your own designs! You may start with a square washcloth or dishcloth, or maybe some rectangular placemats and round coasters to match. You don't need a pattern to do that; just follow your inspiration.

When it's time to design a simple sweater, start with a baby or child size item. It is easier to handle and correct any problems in a smaller size. Make a foundation chain the length of your desired hip measurement. When you think you have enough chains, bring your foundation chain all around the body to be sure of your starting point. Here you can decide whether to have the first and last chain meet for a simple front finish, whether to keep them an inch or so apart to allow for a shell or other trim down the front, or to overlap several chains for a placket that will require a button or similar closure. I usually leave room for trim up and down the front and around the neckline.

Then work on a rectangle to the underarm. This can be as long (such as a coat or long jacket) or as short as you like. I usually allow for bottom trim as well. Use one of your favorite stitches for this part to make it fun! When you decide that your lower section to the underarm is long enough, divide your piece into two fronts and one back section.

This is where you need to count and be certain of your total stitch count. The basic formula is to use half of your stitches in the back and divide the rest for your two front sections, keeping in mind your earlier design decisions.

Sweater Design Practice

For practice, I recommend you make a doll sweater:

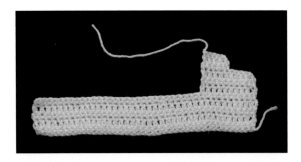

Chain 41, work up 2″ and then in the next row turn your work after 10 stitches, work for 1″ and then turn after 5 stitches for another row or two to make the neckline. Fasten off, leaving a tail for sewing the shoulder seams together.

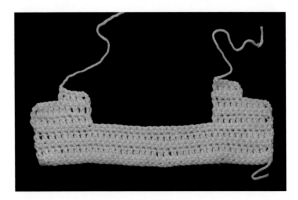

Now skip 20 stitches on the back and connect to the next stitch, work 10 stitches to the end. Now match this side to the opposite side, working the neckline the same way.

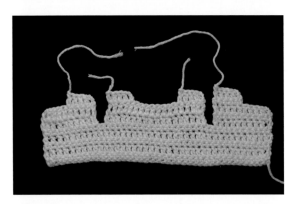

Time to work the back—there are two ways to proceed: You can go into the next stitch from your front or you can skip one stitch, (taking 2 away from the back count) which is nice if you are going to work a sleeve into the arm opening. End your back piece with 5 stitches on each side to meet the fronts for the shoulder seams.

Now fold your fronts towards the back and admire your work. After stitching your shoulder seams together, you can work sleeves directly into the armholes. There are only two seams for the shoulders which is so much easier and quicker than putting bulky seams into your piece.

This simple way to work from the hip up gives you lots of design options. I use this formula for everything from baby items to men's vests. Use any stitch you wish in the main body, and then go for some interesting finishing touches!

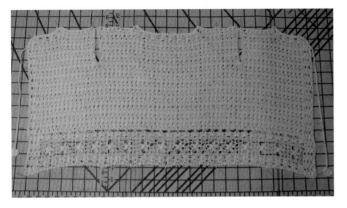

Looks familiar?
Here I am blocking the body of one of my christening coats.

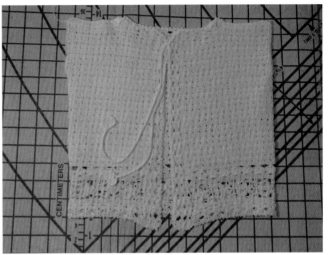

Once the shoulder seams are connected, the sleeves will easily work into the armholes. Lower and center trim complete this piece.

Easy Sleeves That Fit

You can work sleeves directly into the armhole now. On the right side, start at either underarm and work your stitches toward the shoulder. Place one stitch into the shoulder seam and then continue around to the beginning stitch. You will be able to tell if this row is too loose, too tight, or just right. Never pull your stitches too tight here; a bit looser is preferable to being too tight. You can work the sleeves on the right side only or chain and turn each time you complete the row at the underarm, depending on your pattern. After working a few rows you can tell if you need to adjust the number of beginning stitches, or if you are pleased with the fullness.

Be sure to make a note of the number of stitches and rows you used on the first sleeve to get a perfect match for the second one. I always keep a note pad handy; when you are your own designer you need to record certain numbers and reminders!

In the past when using a complicated pattern, sometimes I worked alternately on both sleeves, one row at a time, with both the inside and the outside ends of yarn to keep the pattern even. Now I just make good notes about my progress so I can match the second piece to the original.

When your yarn supply is getting low, you can also work from both ends on your sleeves for example, until you run out of material. This way you can use all of your yarn without any guess work.

Hint

If you are still not comfortable working this way, you may try a paper pattern and work your pieces to fit the paper. Be sure to press the paper with a warm iron to remove any wrinkles, and tape any overlapping seam allowances together.

Paper patterns are handy layout tools if you are working on a freeform piece—they allow you to keep moving any floral or geometric designs on the overall pattern until your final placement is achieved.

Designs in the Round

In my basic coaster instructions you learned the secret of keeping your design flat. Instead of working in continuous rounds, we will now slip stitch to connect at the end of our rows. This way you can switch from one pattern to another in any new row and retain a perfect circle. This is important if you have color changes. The number formula given works for everything from coasters to log cabin size round rugs. You start with your foundation chain of anywhere from 4 to 8 chains, slip stitch into the first chain to close to a ring. Be sure not to twist that foundation chain. Now chain 1 and work 8–16 sc into the ring, doubling the original chain count. Slip stitch to close. Chain 1, now work 2 sc into each sc of the previous row. Connect as before. Now work 1 sc into the next stitch, then 2 sc into the next one, alternate between 1 and 2 sc to the end of the row. Connect as before. In the next row you work 1 sc, 1 sc, 2 sc to the end of the row. From now on just add 1 sc before the 2 sc in each row and your work should stay flat.

When you design and mold the crown of a hat, work your rounds to stay flat until you get to about 5″ or so. Now reduce your increase for a couple of rows and then work into each stitch until you reach the desired length. Add a fun hem or a brim and admire your creation!

HT Original
Mercerized cotton
Here you see the top of my bridal hat;
this was worked in a double crochet and
cluster pattern.

HT Original
Mercerized cotton
Here are other examples of working in the round, increasing stitches for about 5″. Then the hat molds itself once you stop the increases.

71

Side to Side Vertical Designs

Your shoulders always lead the way on vertical designs. Measure across the shoulder from hip or waist front to back to establish your starting length and go from there. It is fun to work a stripe pattern with different colors in this way. You can easily mold your pattern as desired because the lower edge remains even and the opposite edge creates your underarm opening and the neckline as desired.

Be sure to check out the hairpin lace section for more side to side designs.

If you have a dress form it will come in handy. I use mine to leave unfinished vertical design pieces "resting" for a while; it usually sparks more ideas as I see them from the corner of my eye!

Hint

A foldable cardboard cutting board is also a great place to lay out your designs if you put together individual pieces or sections. I have several and use them constantly.

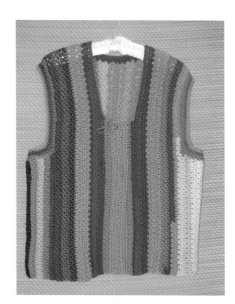

HT Original
Persian embroidery wool
My Fireside Vest was inspired by small amounts of embroidery wool looking for a project. I worked both shoulder strips for several inches, then put them aside. I created a back center section with one hairpin strip, edged with two broomstick rows on each side and then connected to the shoulder strips in the back. Then I proceeded across the underarm and connected to the front of that strip. See how you can control the fit? Now add your front rows as desired and finish with a special touch.

Back detail of Fireside Vest.
You can create interesting details for a great effect or change your design in the center back for some eye catching detail.

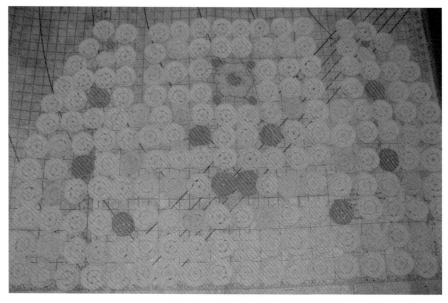

A vest in the making. Here dozens of circles and medallions were laid out to the basic "from the bottom up" rule. The center back features a focal point, other circles of different sizes facilitate the shaping.

Fashion Design Ideas

So, if you love to crochet, try your hand at combining several fun techniques—any time you see loops or stitches, think outside of the box; forget the rules and create something really original. Design an heirloom, like my Mixed Heritage Jacket or a contemporary piece of self-expression, such as my Stitch Galaxy. Only your imagination limits the combination possibilities of nostalgic touches, heritage techniques and contemporary lines.

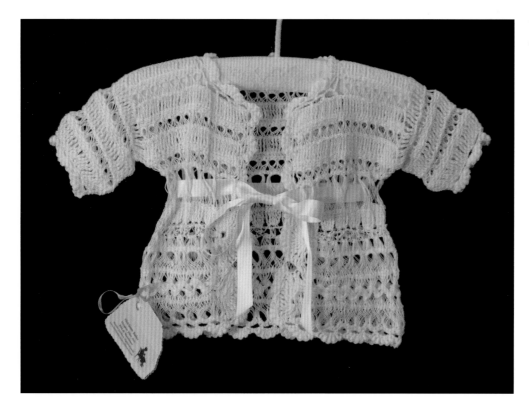

HT Original
A Mixed Heritage Jacket

Here is a great "from the hem up" example:
As you can see, I started with two strips of hairpin lace woven together, followed by two rows of thread lace, and one of double triple crochet, one row of large broomstick lace to accommodate the ribbon, then alternating rows of smaller broomstick lace and more double triple crochets to the shoulders.
The sleeves feature two rows of the smaller broomstick lace, separated by triple crochets. Bullion shells trim the entire piece.
This jacket, like most of my designs, evolved as I worked on it.
Try starting a project with an open mind and let it guide and inspire you as you work with it!

HT Original
Stitch Galaxy Wrap
Nubby Italian cotton
Stitch Galaxy is worked from the top down.

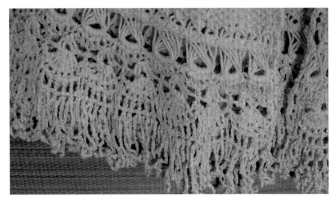

HT Original
This Stitch Galaxy Wrap is made from unbleached, organic Italian cotton and incorporates eight different knit and crochet techniques. From the top down they include hairpin lace, garter stitch knitting, small broomstick lace, large broomstick lace, moss stitch knitting, small and large broomstick lace repeat, thread crochet, and chained fringe, topped with a covered button.

HT Original
Detail of top hairpin row and covered button.

HT Original
Wednesday's Child Sampler Jacket
Italian acrylic blend
This designer piece was created for my Craft Yarn Council's instructor certification. It features Aran cables, front post double crochet diamonds, and trim variations. The jacket is worked in one piece from the hem up and only has shoulder seams. The sleeves are worked into the armholes with a pattern repeat. The ties feature my signature clamshell trim.

Detail of Wednesday's Child front edges.

More Ideas

Of course designing is not limited to wearable art. Many of the hints I gave you will work for other items, such as a tea cozy for your favorite pot. My British friends adore these!

HT Originals
Plain and fancy tea cozies
Start from the top, continue in rounds, turn when you get to the openings, and continue in rounds below the spout and handle for a grand finish!
The fancy version features a twisted cord for adjustment around the knob.
Pair one of these with the Hospitality cake cover in the thread lace section and you are ready for high tea!

Repeat Performance

Last but not least, a word about reusing and recycling.

My mother and grandmother often unraveled older wool and yarn garments out of necessity to reuse the fiber. After they carefully unraveled a few yards, the fiber was loosely wrapped around a wooden bread board, more unraveling and wrapping was done until the board was covered. Then it was soaked in warm, soapy water for a few minutes and then rinsed with running cold water. If they had wool that needed a bit of shrinkage, they used hot water for the soak. After the rinse, the drying usually took several days close to, but not on, the radiator. Since it was wrapped loosely, usually a finger test for dryness between the wood and the fiber was a good indicator if the fiber was ready for the next step.

When completely dry, one of us would hold and turn the board so the fiber could be rolled into a ball. To keep from stretching the fiber, we always had to roll over four fingers and turn the ball frequently for a nice, squeezable finish, much like the skeins on the market now. To this day I enjoy squeezing the commercial skeins of rolled yarn in the yarn aisle! It sure brings back memories!

Many artists now specialize in reusing and recycling available materials. Why not fiber artists?

I seldom use recycled yarn for my projects but when I do I always label a recycled piece accordingly. Mostly I reserve nice pre-owned fiber for my own use. Sometimes for restoration work it is imperative to have a stash of aged or used material to match the pieces of old. So, be sure to keep it all!

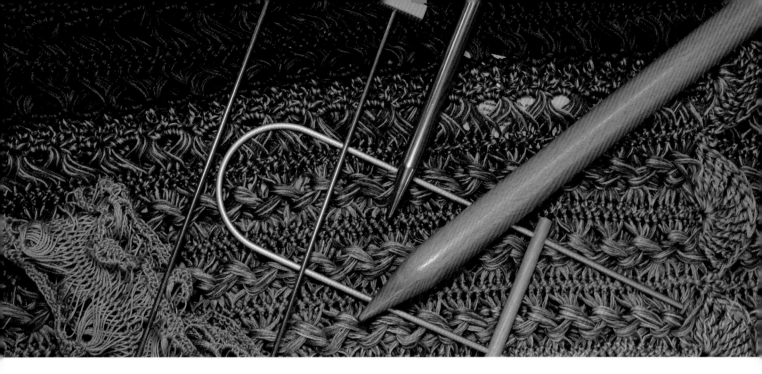

CLOSING THOUGHTS

As you can see, in heritage techniques there is so much more than initially meets the eye — or the hook! Crochet, especially the lace techniques, has come a long way from its origins in the Middle Ages, and through the centuries gathered influences from around the world. Crochet continued in popularity until the start of the First World War, died down, and then resurfaced during the 1960s. Today crochet designs and touches are shown on the runways of many fashion houses. Designers seem to have discovered the romantic link to our past; suddenly what's old is new again! Museums now gather and display extensive collections of crochet, presenting them as wearable art.

Still, crochet in general often has an image problem; many people do not recognize heritage lace tools or completed pieces. We can play a role in saving it from extinction. The bottom line to me and most of my students is that heritage crochet deserves to be practiced and preserved, but let's have fun doing it!

I hope this book inspires you to review old skills or learn some new ones. Most of all I encourage you to find your personal style, be your own designer, and create original pieces that are special to you.

A final note of appreciation goes to Dora Ohrenstein. All this writing and sharing fun started with an invitation by Dora, a well-known crochet designer and instructor who publishes *Crochet Insider Magazine*, to write about heritage techniques for her online magazine. Thank you, Dora Ohrenstein, for being an inspiration to me and to many other crochet artists.

If you are still riding the wave of heritage crochet inspiration, you might enjoy the article from July 2010 in the magazine's archives section:
 http://www.crochetinsider.com/?s=Rita+de+Maintenon

It is fun to look back and see how my love of the work has evolved into being a better teacher and designer.

Thank you for taking this journey with me. Enjoy and pass it on!

Working in my studio.

Here I am shown working as the educational demonstrator at the Folk Art Center on the Blue Ridge Parkway near Asheville, North Carolina. "I do what I love and I love what I do."

INDEX

Growing up in Europe, **Rita de Maintenon** studied and trained in all aspects of fiber work and has taught fiber arts workshops for over twenty years. A retired educator, Rita lives in Asheville, North Carolina, as a full time fiber artist. She has taught heritage fiber classes and workshops for the University of North Carolina at Asheville, the Center for Creative Retirement, the Southeastern Animal Fiber Fair, Arrowmont School of Arts and Crafts, fiber weekend retreats, and local classes. In addition to teaching, Rita loves restoration work on antique pieces and is well known for her designer creations, especially christening gowns. Rita is a member of the Southern Highland Craft Guild and a Blue Ridge National Heritage Artist. She is a Craft Yarn Council certified instructor. Visit her at www.heirloomtreasuresfiberarts.com.